IS 346
Revised January 2003

An Orientation to Hazardous Materials for Medical Personnel

A Self-Study Guide

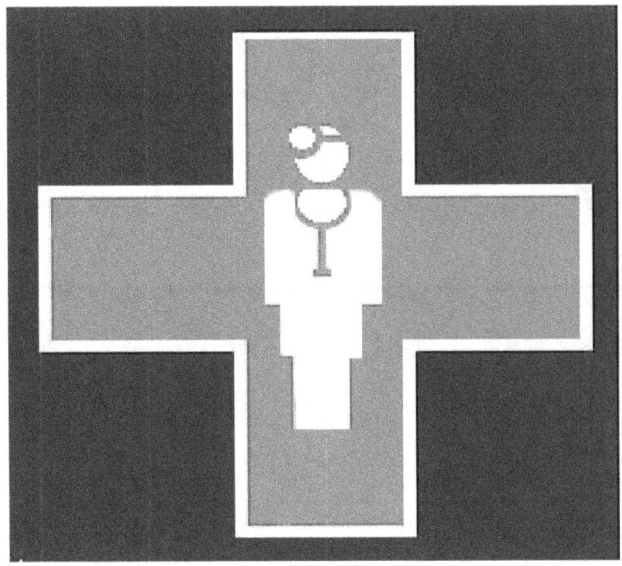

Federal Emergency Management Agency (FEMA)

Table of Contents

UNIT 1:

Introduction

Hospital emergency department personnel face many risks and difficult tasks when dealing with patients involved in hazardous materials incidents. Therefore, it is essential that all personnel who come in contact with patients have a general awareness of the issues and concerns in dealing with hazardous materials incidents. This course is designed to prepare hospital personnel to analyze hazardous materials situations, take the necessary steps to assure medical provider safety, and identify appropriate resources for decontamination and medical care. However, additional training is required in order to diagnose and treat patients who have been involved in hazardous materials incidents. This course alone does not fulfill all of OSHA's requirements for hazardous materials training at the awareness level.

 ## Course Overview

This self-study course is a prerequisite for the *Hospital Emergency Department Management of Hazardous Material Accidents* (HMA) Parts One and Two classroom courses. This course will provide you with a general understanding of the terms and concepts related to hazardous materials and radiation. It also covers some basic principles regarding hospital personnel's response to hazardous materials incidents.

This course, *An Orientation to Hazardous Materials for Medical Personnel,* contains five units, a final examination, and several appendices including a glossary. Words in **boldface** are defined in the Glossary.

Unit 1: Course Introduction

This unit provides details on how to complete the self-study course and an overview of the course. It also describes the medical center or hospital's involvement in hazardous materials events and response efforts, and explains the importance of compliance with federal, state, local, and tribal regulations and standards.

Unit 2: Types and Sources of Hazards

This unit describes the Department of Transportation's hazardous materials classes and identifies the sources of potential hazards in the home, workplace and community. It also describes the possible mechanisms of harm for hazardous materials classes.

Unit 3: Planning for Response

This unit reviews the regulatory requirements regarding medical facilities' and hospitals' emergency/disaster response plans, discusses the staffing resources required to develop a plan and familiarizes you with the basic requirements of a plan.

Unit 4: Responding to Hazards

This unit provides details on how to prepare to receive patients and describes the roles and responsibilities of the key team members of an emergency response team. It also provides details on how to prepare an emergency area and how to prepare the emergency response team. You will also learn about the basic principles regarding hospital emergency department management such as patient assessment and triage, treatment of contaminated patients and decontamination procedures. Finally, this unit describes sources of information on hazardous materials.

Unit 5: Introduction to Radiation

This chapter identifies sources of radiation and presents data on the frequency of radiation accidents. It describes the types of radiation injuries and provides an overview of radiation physics. This unit also describes how to measure radioactivity and the types of instruments used to measure it, defines basic radiation protection principles, and presents the recommended radiation exposure limits. It also covers basic biological effects of ionizing radiation in order to provide a foundation for understanding the clinical aspects of radiation injuries.

Appendices

The appendices include "Chemical/Radiation Event Emergency Plan Addendum," Answer Keys to Exercises, "None/Some/Good Table," a Glossary and a Bibliography. The glossary contains definitions of terms related to hazardous materials and radiation.

 ## Final Examination

The final examination will test the knowledge you have gained from the course.

 ## Intended Audience

This class is designed for hospital emergency department personnel including physicians, nurses, aides, support staff and other emergency medical personnel.

Prerequisites

There are no prerequisites for this course, but a basic understanding of physics and biology is helpful.

 Course Length

This class will take approximately six to ten hours to complete. You can take the course all at once or you can complete the units as time allows.

How To Complete This Course

You can gain more from your self-study learning experience by following these study tips.

- You will remember the material best if you do not rush through it. The more you interact with the material, the better you will be able to remember it! Take a break at the end of each unit and give yourself time to think about the material.

- Do not skip any of the exercises. They are designed to help reinforce your learning and understanding of the terms, concepts and principles presented.

- Most of the units have a pretest that you can take before beginning the unit. If you score 85 percent or higher, you can skip the unit. Each unit is followed by a post-test to check your understanding of the materials. We recommend that you review any questions that you miss by reviewing the topics related to those questions.

- The important terms are highlighted in bold text. If you encounter a term you do not understand, refer to the glossary.

Overview

This unit describes the medical center or hospital's involvement in hazardous materials events and response efforts, and explains the importance of compliance with federal, state, local and tribal regulations and standards.

Objectives

At the conclusion of this unit, you will be able to:

1. Describe the purpose of the course and why it is essential to have the knowledge and skills necessary to recognize and assess situations that can impact the facility and hospital staff in preparing for and responding to hazardous material emergencies.

2. Describe the ways in which a medical center or hospital can be involved in a hazardous material event or response effort.

3. Recognize the importance of compliance with federal, state, local and tribal regulations and standards.

Hospitals' Involvement in Hazardous Materials Events and Response Efforts

There is an increasing concern on the part of medical facilities throughout the nation on how to deal with a hazardous materials response. A hospital's response to a chemical incident may take many forms. Patients, exposed or **contaminated**, may arrive at the emergency department of the medical center or hospital. The facility may find itself in the plume exposure pathway of the release and may have to initiate protective actions. In-place protective efforts, followed by evacuation of the entire facility, may be required.

Disruptions in the community may cause added burdens on the normal medical support provided to the population. As the duration of the threat expands, the complications faced by the medical center increase. Finally, there may be long-term medical effects of the release that require treatment actions or study.

Often, there may be a combination of chemicals involved in the event, or a chemical product may undergo several reactions at the release site creating second or third generation products. Hospitals are often faced with having to identify these hazardous materials and to determine the best treatment approaches. This task is not easy. Most hospital emergency department workers are familiar with dealing with oral poisoning cases. In such events, it may be relatively easy to identify the offending product if the pill bottles or containers with labels with clearly defined descriptions are available. For the lesser known chemicals, hospital workers should become familiar with the Department of Transportation *Emergency Response Guide*. This guide helps you identify the type of substance, but it does not provide treatment solutions. You have to consult other reference documents or poison control centers to determine treatment protocols. Unit 2 contains a listing of resources that you can consult for assistance.

Because the effects of hazardous materials can be devastating and far-reaching, it is important that hospitals cooperate with emergency response groups. It is important to establish a good working relationship with emergency management teams, first responder groups, paramedics, and other groups or individuals actively involved in managing or responding to hazardous materials events.

Patients arriving via EMS may be subject to diversion to a designated hazmat receiving hospital, if an agreement exists. Patients may, however, arrive by private means, and thus will not be subject to diversion policies. The presence of hazardous materials may also not become apparent until after the patient's arrival in the department. Therefore, all emergency departments must be familiar with hazmat, not just those designated to receive patients involved in a hazmat incident.

What Are Hazardous Materials?

Hazardous materials are chemical substances which, if released or misused, can pose a threat to the environment, life or health. Industry, agriculture, medicine, research, and consumer goods use these chemicals. Hazardous materials come in the form of explosives, flammable and combustible substances, poisons, and radioactive materials. These substances are most often released as a result of transportation accidents or chemical accidents in plants.

There are approximately 575,000 existing chemical products, and hundreds of new ones are introduced annually. Varying quantities of hazardous materials are manufactured, used, or stored at approximately 4.5 million facilities in the United States—from major industrial plants to local dry cleaning establishments or gardening supply stores. Most victims of chemical accidents are injured at home. These incidents usually result from ignorance or carelessness in using flammable or combustible materials.

Can Hazardous Materials Cause Harm?

Chemical exposure may cause or contribute to many serious health effects such as heart dysfunction, kidney, lung, and brain damage, sterility, cancer, burns and rashes. Some chemicals may also be safety hazards and have the potential to cause fires and explosions and other serious accidents. According to the U.S. Environmental Protection Agency, radioactive material, a hazardous material, may also be a carcinogen. In this respect, it is similar to many hazardous chemicals found in the environment that can cause cancer.

Sources: *Hazardous Materials Backgrounder*.1993. Document #15092, FEMA Fax Information Line.

Radiation: Risks and Realities, United States Environmental Protection Agency, Air and Radiation, August 1993.

Some Examples of Hazardous Materials Incidents

The following are just some examples of hazardous materials incidents.

- In a small Kentucky community, tank cars containing toxic substances derailed and burned. The fire caused a column of toxic smoke 3,000 feet high that forced 7,500 area residents to evacuate.

- In Florida, vandals broke the valves off several chemical tanks at a local swimming pool supply company. The chemicals mixed to form a toxic acid and a poisonous vapor cloud, sending 45 persons to the hospital.

- In Louisiana, up to 41,000 pounds of hydrobromic acid fouled part of the Mississippi River after two ships collided.

- In Pennsylvania, a garbage truck operator found his load on fire and dumped it in a residential driveway. Mixed chemicals, discarded by a high school science department, released cyanide vapors that sent 100 persons to hospitals.

- Two New Jersey workers were killed and five were injured by vapors inhaled as they cleaned a chemical mixing vat at a local company.

- In 1994, the Department of Transportation reported 16,074 hazardous materials incidents that resulted in 11 deaths and 569 injuries. Nearly 80 percent of the injuries resulted from incidents involving corrosive materials, flammable and combustible liquids, and poisonous materials.

Compliance Issues Regarding Hazardous Materials

There are a number of federal, state, local and tribal regulations and standards that regulate hazardous materials. Following is a brief overview of the major pieces of legislation that are of concern to hospital personnel.

Federal, State, Local, and Tribal Regulations and Standards

Code of Federal Regulations

Part 35 of Title 10 of the Code of Federal Regulations "Medical Use of Byproduct Material" regulates certain use of reactor-produced **radionuclides** used in nuclear medicine and therapeutic radiology. This code requires Nuclear Regulatory Commission (NRC) medical licensees to report medical misadministration events to NRC. The major concerns with the use of radioactive materials in medical applications arise from either a licensee's failure to effectively control a licensed material or from other human errors, such as dispensing a **radiopharmaceutical** that does not comply with a physician's prescription. This can result in a patient receiving an

---

unintended consequence or excessive dose or a dose to the wrong treatment site. Occasionally, the radiopharmaceutical is administered to the wrong patient.

Superfund Amendments and Reauthorization Act of 1986 (SARA)

In 1986, Congress enacted SARA. Title III of the Act, the Emergency Planning and Community Right-to-Know Act of 1986, makes more than 300 "extremely hazardous substances" subject to routine and detailed reporting to designated local, State, and Federal government agencies. It also requires local planning committees to use this information (and other data on local hazards) to create effective plans for hazardous materials emergencies.

The Occupational Safety and Health Act (OSHA)

The Occupational Safety and Health Administration (OSHA) sets standards for worker exposure to hazardous substances and requires that such substances bear warning labels. It also mandates that employees receive training and other information on dangers posed by chemicals, and receive instruction on how to use these chemicals safely. OSHA has the authority to inspect a workplace to determine whether it is in compliance with these regulations.

Under SARA, the Secretary of Labor was directed to issue a final standard to protect the health and safety of employees engaged in hazardous waste operations. In 1989, OSHA issued this rule on Hazardous Waste Operations and Emergency Response, which represents the first comprehensive approach to protecting public and private sector employees involved in the dangerous business of handling hazardous waste materials. Many of the workers affected by this rule are employees of state and local governments. Twenty-five states and territories have their own job safety and health programs. Their standards are required to be at least as stringent as the Federal regulation.

The Toxic Substances Control Act (TSCA)

This legislation was passed in 1976 to reduce the threat from new chemicals that "present or will present an unreasonable risk of injury to human health or the environment." As a result, chemical producers are required to research the effects of new chemicals and notify EPA before they are manufactured. EPA has the authority to ban or restrict chemical uses if there is sufficient evidence that the substance poses an "unreasonable risk."

Federal Agency-Issued Regulations, Standards, and Guidelines

EPA issues standards and guidance to limit human exposure to radiation. The NRC regulates the civilian uses of nuclear materials in the United States by licensing facilities that possess, use, or dispose of byproduct and source material. The NRC also establishes standards governing the activities of licensees and inspects licensed facilities to ensure compliance with its requirements. The Department of Health and Human Services, Food and Drug Administration, Center for Devices and Radiological Health establishes standards for x-ray machines and other electronic products to ensure the protection of human health. The Department of Energy provides technical assistance to States and the private sector in the management and disposal of low-level radioactive waste. The Department of Transportation governs the packaging and transport of hazardous materials and regulates carriers of radioactive materials.

States

The states have agencies responsible for regulating the use of hazardous materials and radiation and for addressing problems and questions. They are the best first source of information about issues that affect their constituents. The states regulate the use of x-ray machines. Some are also licensed to regulate sources of radiation within their state on behalf of EPA, NRC, or OSHA.

 **References**

FEMA, EPA, DOT. 1993. *Hazardous Materials Workshop for Hospital Staff.* Emmitsburg, MD.

U.S. Environmental Protection Agency. 1993. *Radiation: Risks and Realities.* Washington, D.C.

U.S. Nuclear Regulatory Commission. 1994. *Analysis and Evaluation of Operational Data.* Washington, D.C.

UNIT 1: POST-TEST

Directions: Answer each of the following questions. Each item counts 25 points. When you finish,   check your answers in Appendix B. If you missed any items, refer to the applicable sections before   you proceed.

1. Identify three ways in which hospitals may be involved in hazardous materials incidents.

2. Define hazardous materials.

3. List four federal, state or local regulations or standards that regulate hazardous materials.

4. Describe some of the health effects associated with hazardous materials.

UNIT 2:

Types and Sources of Hazards

Overview

In this unit you will learn about the Department of Transportation (DOT) hazardous materials classifications and the sources of potentially hazardous materials in your home, work facility and community. You will also learn how to identify possible mechanisms of injury for hazardous materials classes.

Objectives

At the conclusion of this unit, you will be able to:

1. Describe each of the Department of Transportation (DOT) hazardous materials classifications.

2. Given a situation, identify a possible mechanism of injury for each hazardous materials class.

3. Identify potential hazardous material sources within the home, work facility and the community.

Pretest

If you think you have the requisite skills and knowledge for this topic area, take the pretest on the next page. If you score within the passing range of 85%, you can skip this unit and proceed to unit three.

UNIT 2: PRETEST

Purpose: To assess your knowledge of the types and sources of hazards, the Department of Transportation hazardous materials classes, and the potential mechanisms of injury from hazardous materials.

Directions: Read each item and answer it.

(If you score within the passing range of 85%, you can skip this unit and proceed to unit three. Do not check the Answer Key (Appendix B) until after you have completed the test.)

PART I

1. Match the DOT hazardous materials classifications with the correct description. (Each answer counts 10 points.)

DOT Hazardous Materials Classification	Description
_____1. Corrosive Materials	a. A chemical that causes a sudden, almost instantaneous release of pressure, gas and heat when subjected to sudden shock, pressure or high temperatures.
_____2. Radioactive Materials	b. Solids likely to cause fires through friction or retained heat from manufacturing or processing or that are easy to ignite, such as matches.
_____3. Flammable Solids	c. Materials that readily yield oxygen to support combustion.
_____4. Oxidizers	d. Liquids or solids that damage human tissue or steel on contact, such as sulfuric acid.
_____5. Explosives	e. Substances that emit alpha and beta particles or gamma rays spontaneously.

PART II

2. List four for mechanisms of harm from hazardous materials. (Each answer counts 5 points.)

    a.

    b.

    c.

    d.

3. List six sources of potential hazardous materials within the home, work facility and community.   (Each answer counts 5 points.)

    a.

    b.

    c.

    d.

    e.

    f.

Department of Transportation (DOT) Hazardous Materials Classifications

The United Nations (UN) and the U.S. Department of Transportation (DOT) have devised a way to classify hazardous materials based on the chemical and physical properties of the product that is referred to as a hazard class. Each of these classes is then broken down into specific subsets. For example, gases may be poisonous, flammable, or nonflammable. Oxygen and chlorine are gases that have their own individual labels. Each class has a symbol that suggests the *primary* type of hazard it poses.

Each class has a symbol that suggests the *primary* type of hazard it poses. This DOT system is catalogued in *The Emergency Response Guidebook*, compiled by the Department of Transportation, Research and Special Programs Administration, and published by the U.S. Government Printing Office and numerous distributors. A current copy should be readily accessible in your facility. *Can you locate a copy of this guidebook in your hospital?*

The hazard class of dangerous goods is indicated either by its class (or division) number or name. For a placard corresponding to the primary hazard class of a material, the hazard class or division number must be displayed in the lower corner of the placard. However, no hazard class or division number may be displayed on a placard representing the subsidiary hazard of a material. For other than Class 7 or the OXYGEN placard, text indicating a hazard (for example, "CORROSIVE") is not required. Text is shown only in the U.S. The hazard class or division number must appear on the shipping document after each shipping name.

The nine DOT Hazard Classes are summarized below.

Class 1—Explosives

Division 1.1	**Explosives with a mass explosion hazard**
Division 1.2	**Explosives with a projection hazard**
Division 1.3	**Explosives with predominantly a fire hazard**
Division 1.4	**Explosives with no significant blast hazard**
Division 1.5	**Very insensitive explosives; blasting agents**
Division 1.6	**Extremely insensitive detonating articles**

A chemical that causes a sudden, almost instantaneous release of pressure, gas and heat when subjected to sudden shock, pressure, or high temperatures. These explosives have thermal and mechanical impact potential.

Division 1.1—Explosives that will detonate, burn at 1,250 feet per second, and produce a shockwave. *Examples*: dynamite, blasting caps, and most military explosives.

Division 1.2—Explosives that burn rapidly, but at less than 1,250 feet per second. *Examples*: special fireworks, liquid rocket propellants, and flash powders.

Division 1.3—Explosives that have a fire hazard and either a minor blast hazard or a minor projection hazard or both, but not a mass explosion hazard. *Examples*: most fireworks, small arms ammunition, safety fuses, and paper caps.

Division 1.4—Explosives that present a minor explosion hazard, such as ammunition.

Division 1.5—Explosives that have a mass explosion hazard but are so insensitive that there is very little probability of irritation, such as ammonium nitrate.

Division 1.6—Extremely insensitive articles that do not have a mass explosion hazard, such as fuel oil.

Class 2—Gases

Division 2.1	**Flammable gases**
Division 2.2	**Nonflammable, non-toxic* compressed gases**
Division 2.3	**Gases toxic* by inhalation**
Division 2.4	**Corrosive gases (Canada)**

Gases are grouped into three types: compressed, liquefied, and cryogenic. Gas can be flammable, nonflammable and poisonous. These gases can vaporize, which could cause respiratory problems, burn to cause thermal-related injuries, or cause frostbite due to exceedingly cold temperatures.

Division 2.1—Flammable gases such as propane, methane, and hydrogen.

Division 2.2—Nonflammable gases, non-toxic compressed gases such as neon, helium, and carbon dioxide. Their primary hazard is cylinder failure when stored under pressure.

Division 2.3—Poison gases by inhalation. May be gases that vaporize easily, and that are very dangerous to life, even in small amounts. *Examples*: cyanide, hydrocyanic acid and diphosgene. Other gases include oxygen and chlorine.

Class 3—Flammable liquids (and Combustible liquids [U.S.])

These materials will burn, but will require an ignition source. DOT Flammable liquids have flashpoint below 141°F. *Examples*: gasoline and alcohol. Combustible liquid requires heating, and range between 141° – 200°F. *Examples*: pine oil, fuel oil, and plastic solvents.

Class 4—Flammable solids; Spontaneously combustible materials; and Dangerous when wet materials

Division 4.1   Flammable solids

Division 4.2   Spontaneously combustible materials

Division 4.3   Dangerous when wet materials

These solids are potentially corrosive, toxic, and thermally unstable.

Division 4.1—Flammable solids: Solids likely to cause fires through friction or retained heat from manufacturing or processing or that are easy to ignite. *Examples*: matches or sulfur.

Division 4.2—Spontaneously combustible materials: A material that ignites spontaneously upon exposure to air (or oxygen). Also called pyrophoric materials (spontaneously ignite at or below 130°F).

Division 4.3—Dangerous when wet materials: Solid materials that, when in contact with water or organic substances, may initiate or intensify fires. They can produce significant toxic gas when they come in contact with water, or react violently. *Examples*: potassium, sodium, aluminum, or magnesium.

Class 5—Oxidizers and Organic peroxides

Division 5.1	Oxidizers
Division 5.2	**Organic peroxides**

These materials are potentially toxic.

Division 5.1—Oxidizers: Materials (in the form of gases, liquids, or solids) that readily yield oxygen to support combustion. This could include gases such as oxygen, ozone, or chlorine; liquids such as bromine, hydrogen peroxide, and nitric acid; and solids such as chlorates, iodine, nitrates, and peroxides.

Division 5.2—Organic peroxides: Flammable compounds (liquids, pastes, and solids) which contain the double oxygen or perxoy (-O-O-) group, that are subject to explosive decomposition. Some examples of organic peroxides are t-butyl hydroperoxide, acetyl peroxide, peroxyacetic acid, benzoyl peroxide, and lauroyl peroxide.

Class 6—Toxic* materials and Infectious substances

Division 6.1   **Toxic* materials**

Division 6.2   **Infectious substances**

Harm can occur from inhalation, ingestion, or absorption.

Division 6.1—Toxic materials: Poisons that pose a serious health hazard to humans. *Examples*: parathion and potassium arsenate.

Division 6.2—Infectious substances: Living organisms or their toxins that can cause disease in humans. *Examples:* anthrax, botulism and the polio virus.

Class 7—Radioactive materials

Any material that spontaneously emits ionizing radiation and that has specific activity greater than 0.002 microcuries per gram. Depending on exposure, can be fatal or cause serious harm to internal organs and cause long-term effects that can result in cancer.

Class 8—Corrosive materials

Liquids or solids that damage human tissue or steel on contact. *Examples*: sulfuric acid, nitric acid and ammonium hydroxide.

Class 9—Miscellaneous dangerous goods

Division 9.1   **Miscellaneous dangerous goods (Canada)**

Division 9.2   **Environmentally hazardous substances (Canada)**

Division 9.3   **Dangerous wastes (Canada)**

A material that presents a hazard during transportation, but which does not meet the definition of any other hazard class. This class includes any material that has an anesthetic, noxious or other similar property that could cause annoyance or discomfort and any materials that meet the definitions for an elevated temperature material, a hazardous substance, or a hazardous waste. Some materials found in this class include carbon dioxide (dry ice), cotton, lead sulfite, lithium batteries, life-saving appliances, and zinc dithionite. Such materials can be toxic or corrosive.

* The words "poison" or "poisonous" are synonymous with the word "toxic."

Mechanisms of Injury for Hazardous Materials

Hazardous materials are capable of harming people, property, and the environment.

How Hazardous Materials Harm the Body

Toxic substances can enter our bodies through four routes of entry: absorption, injection, ingestion and inhalation. Each of these four routes is described in the table below.

Routes of Entry into the Body for Hazardous Materials
Absorption (through the skin or eye). Some hazardous materials can be absorbed through the skin (epidermal cells, sweat glands, sebaceous glands, or hair follicles). For example, if you walk on contaminated soil, you risk some type of exposure; breaks in the skin or ulcers increase the risk because absorption occurs faster. The eyes can also absorb chemicals very quickly, either through a direct splash to the eye or through toxic smoke particles in the air or absorption of vapors or toxic gases.
Injection. Hazardous materials may enter the body accidentally through a puncture wound such as when a contaminated glass cuts the skin. Other injections—such as a needle—may be deliberate, though not intentionally harmful. With injections, the hazardous material enters the bloodstream almost immediately.
Ingestion. You can come in contact with hazardous materials through smoking or eating. You may accidentally eat food that has been in contact with a harmful substance, or you could accidentally eat or drink a harmful substance. Residue from chemicals on food may also be ingested. Material may splash, spray, etc. on the mouth or nose.
Inhalation. You can breathe toxic substances or gases into your lungs. Highly water-soluble gases, such as ammonia, hydrogen chloride, and hydrogen fluoride, are quickly dissolved in the mucous membranes of the nose and upper respiratory tract, which can cause irritation. Insoluble substances may be deposited in the lungs, causing local toxicity.

Regardless of the many things that can happen, the mechanisms of harm fall into seven types of causes: thermal, etiologic, asphyxiant, mechanical, chemical, psychological, and radiological.

Thermal. Thermal refers to those events related to temperature extremes. High temperatures are common at fire-related incidents, but we often forget or ignore the potential for injury from extreme cold.

Etiologic. Etiologic refers to uncontrolled exposure to living, disease-causing microorganisms. Diseases commonly associated with etiologic harm include hepatitis, typhoid fever, and a number of influenza viruses. Some of the more frightening etiologic agents are associated with germ warfare.

Asphyxiant. Many materials can displace oxygen when released in confined environments; among them are nitrogen, carbon dioxide, and natural gas. Asphyxiation can occur when chemicals interfere with the respiratory process. For example, carbon monoxide reduces the oxygen-carrying ability of the blood, and cyanide prevents oxygen from being used by body tissues.

Mechanical. Some chemicals produce "mechanical" injury leading to tissue damage and cell death. For example, sulfuric acid can cause violent dehydration of cells because of its strong attraction to water. Mechanical can also refer to injuries caused by shock waves, impact forces, or the scattering of debris such as from shrapnel in an explosion or a blast. This avenue of harm must be considered in the light of possible contamination as well as injury. The lacerations or punctures to the skin from a mechanical agent can lead to complications if injurious substances penetrate the skin.

Chemical. Most hazardous chemicals cause injury by reacting with body tissues to alter the structure or function of cells and their components. For example, exposure to a corrosive substance such as nitric acid can cause severe and deep tissue burns or permanent eye damage. Hydrofluoric acid can cause bone damage, whereas anhydrous ammonia causes internal burns, and parathion damages the nervous system.

Psychological. Though not a direct outcome of contact with a hazardous material, psychological factors can be a mechanism of harm. Stress is a frequent outcome of responding to such events.

Radiological. Energy released from radioactive sources such as **alpha**, **beta** or **gamma** radiation can do serious harm to the body. Often, these harmful results can be long lasting and can lead to death. You will learn more details about radiation in unit 5.

It is important to understand the mechanisms of harm in order to properly diagnose and treat individuals who have come in contact with hazardous materials.

✓ **Exercise: Identifying Mechanisms of Harm Effects on the Body**

Purpose: To determine which body system can be injured by each mechanism of harm.

Directions: Using the matrix below, indicate those mechanisms of harm that could affect each of the eight bodily systems. You can check your answers in Appendix B.

Mechanism of Harm Effects

Body System	Thermal	Etiologic	Asphyxiant	Mechanical	Chemical	Psychological	Radiological
Neurological							
Respiratory							
Circulatory							
Reproductive							
Musculoskeletal							
Digestive							
Skin							
Renal							

Sources of Hazards

Hazardous materials incidents can occur anytime and anywhere in the United States or your community. While we often associate our hazardous materials problems with industry, there are numerous sources of hazards. The table below describes the most prevalent sources of hazards.

Sources of Hazards
 **Transportation Incidents** Hazardous materials are transported daily in the United States by air, water, road, rail, and pipeline. Of the 1.5 billion tons of hazardous materials transported in this country each year, more than half move by tankers along the nation's highways. Hazardous materials may spill, explode, or burn due to accidents involving railways, trucks, and ships. Most hazardous materials transportation accidents involve flammable or combustible liquids, such as gasoline and fuel oil. The second most frequent type of incident involves corrosives materials.
Fixed Facilities and Storage Fixed installation accidents can occur anywhere hazardous materials are manufactured, processed, used, transported, or stored. These accidents may occur due to human error, equipment failure, accidental mixing of reactive products, physical damage to containers, or exposure to fire, water, or heat. Hazardous materials are stored before and after they are transported to their intended use. For example, service stations store gasoline and diesel fuel in underground tanks; hospitals store radioactive isotopes, flammable materials, and other hazardous substances; and manufacturers store a variety of chemicals on site.
Hazardous Materials Waste Sites Hazardous waste sites affect many communities across the country. These include abandoned dump sites, municipal landfills, industrial ponds, storage piles, military base waste sites, and similarly designated areas. There are approximately 22,000 hazardous waste sites identified by the Environmental Protection Agency. The most common form of contamination at a landfill site is **toxic leachate**. Formed as rainwater percolates down through a landfill, leachate carries soluble toxic and hazardous materials absorbed from the garbage downward through the soil.

Medical Procedures

Radiation exposure occurs in diagnostic x-rays and radiopharmaceuticals.

Consumer Products

Toxic chemicals are stored in almost every room of a typical American home: cleansers in the kitchen, fresheners in the bathroom, and hobby supplies in the workroom, to name but a few. In an average city of 100,000 residents, 23.5 tons of toilet bowl cleaner, 13.5 tons of liquid household cleaners, and 3.5 tons of motor oil are discharged into city drains each month, according to the Environmental Hazards Management Institute. These figures do **not** reflect the large quantities of household hazardous wastes disposed of in backyards. In addition, improper disposal of hazardous waste from these household products can contaminate our land, water, and air.

Naturally Occurring Toxic Substances

Radiation occurs naturally through cosmic radiation, from the earth, and from building materials. Radon, a source of radiation, is a colorless, odorless gas that comes from the decay of uranium found in nearly all soils. There are also trace elements in human tissues.

 ### Automobiles

Automobiles emit nitrous oxides (one source of "acid rain") and several air toxins.

Soil

Soil may become contaminated through dumping, spills and other sources. Rainwater leaches some contaminants from the soil and carries them to groundwater. Other contaminants remain near the surface, where they can affect human health by entering the food chain (ingestion) or rubbing onto the skin of children playing in the dirt (dermal absorption).

Air

Hazardous chemicals can enter the atmosphere from a point source (such as an industrial stack) or from an area source (such as the evaporation of volatile compounds from hazardous waste sites).

Ground Water and Surface Water

Hazardous materials may spill into the water and contaminate it. Contamination can occur when industrial waste and sewage discharges into the water, or when hazardous waste landfills leak into the water.

✔ Exercise: Identify Sources of Hazardous Materials in Your Community

Purpose: To become acquainted with the sources of hazards that may pose problems in your community.

Directions: Seek out information from your facility security or safety officer, the local emergency management office, or other resources to identify *at least five* sources of hazardous materials in
your community.

1.

2.

3.

4.

5.

6.

7.

8.

9.

10.

 **References**

FEMA, NFA. 1995. *Basic Life Support and Hazardous Materials Response.* Emmitsburg, MD.

FEMA, EMI. *Hazardous Materials: A Citizen's Orientation Independent Study Course.* Emmitsburg, MD.

FEMA Fax Information Line. 1993. *Hazardous Materials Backgrounder*, Document #15092.

United States Environmental Protection Agency. August, 1993. *Radiation: Risks and Realities*, Air and Radiation.

Unit 2: POST-TEST

Directions: Answer each question. *Check your answers in Appendix B after you have finished the test. If you missed any items, review the applicable sections before you proceed.*

PART I: Match the DOT hazardous classes with the appropriate description. Each answer counts 10 points.

DOT Hazardous Class	Description
_____ 1. Flammable Gas	a. Anthrax, botulism and polio virus.
_____ 2. Flammable Liquid	b. Flammable compounds that contain the double oxygen or perxoy group that are subject to explosive decomposition.
_____ 3. Organic Peroxide	c. Matches or sulfur.
_____ 4. Etiologic or Infectious Organism	d. Propane, methane and hydrogen.
_____ 5. Flammable Solid	e. Liquids with a flashpoint below 100 degrees F.

PART II: Match the potential mechanisms for harm to their causes. Each answer counts 10 points.

Cause	Potential Harm
_____ 1. Etiologic	a. Fireworks explode unexpectedly, causing burns over 30 percent of the body.
_____ 2. Asphyxiant	b. You are exposed to hepatitis on your visit to Malaysia.
_____ 3. Radiological	c. Your basement contains excessive amounts of radon.
_____ 4. Chemical	d. You spill nitric acid and it splashes into your eyes.
_____ 5. Thermal	e. Your gas heater malfunctions and emits dangerous levels of carbon monoxide.

UNIT 3:

Planning for Response

Overview

This unit reviews the regulatory requirements regarding medical facilities' and hospitals' emergency/disaster response plans, discusses the staffing resources required to develop a plan and familiarizes you with the basic requirements of a plan.

Objectives

At the end of this unit, you will be able to:

1. Describe the need for a hospital emergency/disaster response plan.

2. Identify who should be involved in the development, implementation and evaluation of the hospital emergency/disaster plan.

3. Locate and review the hospital's emergency/disaster response plan.

4. Use a sample hospital emergency/disaster response plan to:

   a) Identify procedures for facility and personnel contamination control.
   b) Identify the primary and secondary areas for patient reception triage and decontamination treatment.
   c) Identify personnel for response duties.
   d) Define roles and responsibilities of personnel.
   e) Identify safety and security precautions.

Pretest

If you think you have the requisite skills and knowledge for this topic area, take the pretest below. If you score within the passing range of 85%, you can skip this unit and proceed to unit four.

UNIT 3: PRETEST

Purpose: This pretest will assess your knowledge of hospital emergency/disaster response plans.

Directions: Read and answer each item. Each answer counts 20 points.

(If you score within the passing range of 85%, you can skip this unit and proceed to unit four. Do not check the Answer Key (Appendix B) until after you have completed the pretest.)

1. What is the purpose of a hospital emergency/disaster response plan?

2. List five individuals or agencies that should be involved in the development of a hospital's emergency/disaster response plan.
   a.
   b.
   c.
   d.
   e.

3. List five basic elements that should be included in the hospital's emergency/disaster response plan.
   a.
   b.
   c.
   d.
   e.

4. Why is it important to have a hospital emergency/disaster response plan?

5. What is the name or title of the individual who is responsible for the overall development of your hospital's emergency/disaster response plan?

The Hospital Emergency/Disaster Response Plan

There is an increasing concern on the part of medical facilities throughout the nation on how to deal with hazardous materials response. Proper planning for emergencies is necessary to minimize employee injury and property damage. The hospital's emergency/disaster response plan is a critical document in ensuring that the hospital or medical facility is prepared to respond to hazardous materials incidents. The hospital emergency/disaster plan describes the policies and guidelines to follow in the event of a hazardous materials incident. Hospitals' emergency/disaster response plans will vary, but there are certain minimum requirements that any plan should meet. These requirements are specified, in part, by the following:

- Current Joint Commission for the Accreditation of Healthcare Organizations (JCAHO) *Accreditation Manual for Hospitals*
- National Fire Codes
- The community emergency preparedness plan
- Community fire and sanitation ordinances
- Applicable state and federal regulations

When developing your plan, you should consult the latest version of the JCAHO *Accreditation Manual for Hospitals* to obtain information on the basic requirements for the emergency preparedness program. The table below presents some of the requirements central to any hospital emergency/disaster response plan.

Some Basic Requirements for a Hospital Emergency/Disaster Response Plan

- Roles and responsibilities of the hospital and staff
- Organizational and reporting structure in an emergency
- Fire plan
- Guidelines and policies for access to emergency care areas
- Communications systems alternatives (when main communication system fails)
- Guidelines to follow when electrical, air conditioning, plumbing, boiler systems, and essential life support systems fail
- Guidelines for patient management (scheduling, modification, discontinuation of services, control of patient information, and admission, transfer, and discharge of patients)
- Evacuation plan
- Special equipment requirements (for hazardous materials incidents)

The plan should be updated continuously to ensure that all information is up-to-date and accurate.

Unit 3: Planning for Response

Basic Components of the Plan

Though the exact format of the disaster/emergency response plan will vary, it will usually consist of the following components:

- The **basic plan**, which is a relatively broad conceptual framework describing the policy and approach to emergency operations.

- **Supporting annexes** that contain information on specific functional responsibilities, tasks, and operational actions needed to deal with particular hazards. The focus of an annex is on operations—what the function is and how it is carried out. Annexes are action-oriented and written for personnel charged with executing the plan. Examples of annexes include warning, evacuation, and fire and rescue. Because the requirements of hazardous materials incidents differ markedly from those of other emergencies, a separate hazardous materials annex to the generic operations plan is needed to address these issues.

- **Implementing guidelines**—these may be in the form of hazard-specific appendices, standard operating guidelines or checklists. They support annexes and contain technical and detailed operational information for use by emergency personnel, including such information as lists of people to alert under specified conditions and specific "how to" instructions for operating departments or individuals to carry out assigned responsibilities.

 Exercise: Locate Your Hospital's Emergency/Disaster Response Plan

Does your hospital have an emergency/disaster response plan?

Locate a copy of the plan because you will need it later to complete an exercise.

The Importance of an Emergency/Disaster Response Plan

The effectiveness of response during emergencies depends on the amount of planning and training performed. During hazardous materials incidents, many additional burdens may be placed on a medical facility. Medical facilities may be receiving potentially contaminated or exposed patients who may require immediate actions and perhaps isolation or **decontamination**. In addition, persons evacuating their homes may forget to take the medications they need for chronic conditions. Such patients will often end up in the emergency department because they do not have their medication or failed to take it in the required time period. The stress effects of hazardous materials incidents can cause an increase in such medical conditions as cardiac problems, premature births, traffic accidents, and other stress-related symptoms. When all of these incidents are compounded, a facility can be overwhelmed quickly—unless detailed procedures for handling such incidents are available and readily accessible.

Personnel Involved in Developing, Implementing, and Evaluating an Emergency/Disaster Response Plan

Management must show its support for hospital safety programs and emergency planning. It is, therefore, management's responsibility to see that a program is instituted and to ensure that the program is reviewed and updated frequently. The input and support of all employees should be obtained to ensure an effective program. The primary goal should be to include representatives from all departments that may be involved in responding to a hazardous materials incident. Because your response to hazardous materials events may involve close coordination with outside officials and organizations, you should also include representatives from community organizations and local emergency response agencies.

For example, under the provisions of the Superfund Amendments and Reauthorization Act, Local Emergency Planning Committees (LEPCs) have been established to develop a community-wide emergency response plan for dealing with a chemical release. The law requires that medical personnel be a part of the LEPC membership.

Unit 3: Planning for Response

The table below lists some of the personnel who should be involved in the development of the plan.

Personnel Involved in Developing an Emergency/Disaster Response Plan	
Hospital Personnel	**Other Personnel/Agencies**
• Medical staff • Nursing administrator • Facility engineer • Housekeeping services representative • Food service administrator • Emergency department administrator • Security officer • Risk management advisor • Public affairs representative • Communications representative • Safety director • Senior management representatives	• Field Emergency Medical Service providers • Fire and law enforcement officials • Representatives of the Local Emergency Planning Committee • Red Cross and human service agencies • Hazardous materials response teams • 911 and emergency dispatch centers • Poison Control Centers • Air ambulance services • Other hospital and medical centers • Public health agencies • Visiting Nurse Associations

During the development of the plan, it is important to remember that it is the planning process, not the creation of the paper document, that is important. Once the plan is prepared and personnel are trained in their respective functions, it is important to exercise the system. The purpose of an effective exercise program is to learn where planning and coordination flaws exist so that corrections can be made.

The emergency/disaster response plan should be developed locally and should be comprehensive enough to deal with all types of hazardous materials emergencies.

Each hospital should designate one individual with overall responsibility for the hospital emergency/disaster response plan. This individual most likely will have dual responsibilities and may have another title, such as director of nursing or safety director.

Do you know who has overall responsibility for the hospital emergency/disaster response plan? Write his or her name here.

Using the Hospital Emergency/Disaster Response Plan

The hospital emergency/disaster response plan can be a complex document; therefore, it is important for you to become familiar with the document—before a disaster strikes. The following exercise will help you become familiar with your hospital's plan (or if you do not have one available, the sample plan).

✔ Exercise: Interpreting the Hospital Emergency/Disaster Response Plan

Purpose: To become acquainted with a hospital emergency/disaster response plan.

Directions: Use your hospital's emergency/disaster response plan to answer the following questions. If you do not have a plan, use the sample plan in Appendix A.

---

1. Locate the section that identifies the personnel for response duties.

2. Locate the section that defines the roles and responsibilities of personnel.

3. Locate the section(s) that identifies the primary and secondary areas for patient reception triage and decontamination treatment.

4. Locate the section(s) that identifies safety and security precautions that should be followed.

5. Locate the section(s) that identifies procedures for facility and personnel contamination control.

 **References**

Beatty, G. C. 1987. *Developing a Hospital Emergency Preparedness Program.* Chicago: American Hospital Association.

FEMA, EPA, DOT. 1993. *Hazardous Materials Workshop for Hospital Staff.* Emmitsburg, MD.

Unit 3: Planning for Response

Directions: Answer each of the questions below.

(Check your answers in Appendix B. If you missed any items, you should review this unit before proceeding).

1.   Which of the following documents would contain the policies and procedures that *you* should follow in your facility in responding to a hazardous materials incident?

   a)   JCAHO Accreditation Manual for Hospitals
   b)   Your hospital's emergency/disaster response plan
   c)   The state's code of regulations
   d)   The community emergency preparedness plan

2.   Which of the following is not a basic component of the hospital's emergency/disaster response plan?

   a)   Basic plan
   b)   Supporting annexes
   c)   Implementing guidelines
   d)   Community fire and building codes

3.   Who should be involved in the development of the hospital's emergency/disaster response plan?

   a)   Only management representatives from each department in the hospital
   b)   All employees, including management and representatives from every department who may be involved in responding to a hazardous materials incident
   c)   Just emergency physicians and nurses
   d)   Primarily, the hospital administrator and security personnel

4.   What is the purpose of the hospital's emergency/disaster response plan?

   a)   To provide details on how to control the spread of fires in the event of an emergency
   b)   To provide job descriptions for hospital personnel
   c)   To describe the policies and guidelines to follow in the event of a hazardous materials incident
   d)   To identify the community's fire and sanitation ordinances

UNIT 4:

Responding to Hazards

Overview

This unit provides details on how to prepare to receive a patient(s) and describes the roles and responsibilities of the key team members of an emergency response team. It also provides details on how to prepare an emergency area and how to prepare the emergency response team. You will also review the basic principles of hospital emergency department management, such as patient assessment and triage, treatment of contaminated patients and decontamination procedures. Finally, this unit describes sources of information on hazardous materials.

Objectives

At the conclusion of this unit, you will be able to:

1. Describe some of the key requirements involved in the reception of a patient contaminated or exposed to a hazardous chemical, radiological or etiologic substance.

2. Discuss the functions of various members of the hazardous materials emergency response team.

3. Identify three reasons for the need for special preparation techniques in the emergency area.

4. List at least three ways to prepare the emergency area for receipt of patients to control the spread of hazardous materials and ensure staff safety.

5. Identify suitable personal protection equipment for responding to a hazardous materials incident.

6. Describe the basic procedures for patient assessment and triage.

7. Describe the basic procedures for treatment of a contaminated patient.

8. Identify types of radiological and clinical laboratory assessments required and state reasons why they are required.

9. Describe the purpose of decontamination and the basic components of the decontamination process.

10. Define seven common decontamination mechanisms.

11. List and describe the hospital's hazardous materials information resources and ensure that they are authoritative and up to date.

Pretest

If you think you have the requisite skills and knowledge for this topic area, take the pretest on the next page. If you score at or above the passing range of 85%, skip this unit and proceed to unit five.

UNIT 4: PRETEST

Purpose: This pretest will assess your knowledge about issues and procedures in responding to hazardous materials incidents.

Directions: Read each item and answer accordingly. Each answer counts 20 points. *(If you score at*
or above the passing range of 85%, skip this unit and proceed to unit five. Do not check the Answer
Key (Appendix B) until after you have completed the test.)

1. When someone or something else comes in contact with someone or something else that has been contaminated, this is known as:
    a) cross contamination
    b) direct contamination
    c) residual contamination
    d) gross contamination

2. Removing a major amount but not all of the contaminant from the contaminated person or object is an example of:
    a) secondary decontamination
    b) gross decontamination
    c) full-stage decontamination
    d) level A decontamination

3. Chemical alteration of a hazardous material into a harmless substance is called _____.
    a) dilution
    b) degradation
    c) disinfection
    d) absorption

4. Which of the following is not a technique for contamination control?
    a) Monitor anyone or anything that leaves the controlled area.
    b) Control ventilation.
    c) Set up a controlled area large enough to hold the anticipated number of victims.
    d) Register all victims at the reception desk before sending them to the decontamination area.

5. List five members of the emergency response team.

Preparing To Receive the Patient

Any hazardous materials event requires a coordinated effort to ensure that all variables are addressed. The emergency response team is an essential component in an effective response, but the initial response begins with accident notification and verification.

Notification and Accident Verification

When the hospital receives a call that a hazardous material incident has occurred and that affected patient(s) will be admitted, the call-taker should get as much information as possible. An effective response cannot occur without accurate and complete information. At a minimum, the following should be standard requirements:

- Number of accident victims
- Each victim's medical status and triage category
- Whether victims have been surveyed for **contamination**
- For radiation incidents, the radiological status of the victims (exposed versus contaminated)
- Identity of contaminant, if known
- Estimated time of arrival
- Call-back number for verification

Medical personnel responding to emergency event calls should assume the victim is contaminated until proven otherwise and base their actions on that assumption. They should advise ambulance personnel of any special entrance requirements.

Contamination vs. Decontamination

Contamination: Substance capable of causing harm to life, health or the environment is physically deposited on the person, animal or object. When the substance (liquid, solid or vapor) actually touches the body or thing, direct or primary contamination occurs. A person or item that has been exposed to a hazardous material is **contaminated** and can contaminate other people or items (called **cross-contamination**). For example, if you enter your car after being exposed to a toxic substance, you will contaminate your car.

Decontamination: The process of removing or neutralizing contaminants that have accumulated on people and equipment.

 **The Emergency Response Team**

The emergency response team consists of a number of individuals, each of whom plays a critical role in a successful response. Though the exact composition of the emergency response team will vary from facility to facility, the following members are usually a part of the emergency response team. In addition, the hospital emergency response team must coordinate its efforts with field personnel and the incident commander involved in handling the events. The composition of the team and the numbers of people needed will vary depending on the magnitude of the response. Team positions may be combined in a smaller scale response. In a large-scale response, the team may need to expand.

Emergency Response Team Members	
Team Member	**Function (Roles and Responsibilities)**
Team Coordinator	Leads, advises, coordinates.
Emergency Physician	Diagnoses, treats and provides emergency medical care; can also function as team coordinator or triage officer.
Triage Officer	Performs triage.
Nurse	Assists physician with medical procedures, collection of specimens, radiological monitoring, where applicable, and decontamination. Assesses patient needs and intervenes appropriately.
Technical Recorder	Records and documents medical data (and, where applicable, specific data regarding hazardous materials).
Safety Officer (or Radiation Safety Officer)	Monitors patient and area and advises on contamination and exposure control; maintains survey equipment.
Public Information Officer	Releases accident information to the media.
Administrator	Coordinates hospital response and assures normal hospital operations.
Security Personnel	Secure the emergency area and control crowds.
Maintenance Personnel	Aid in preparation of the emergency area for contamination control, where applicable.
Laboratory Technician	Provides routine clinical analysis of biological samples and others as required.

 **Exercise: Who's Responsible for What?**

Purpose: To assess your knowledge of the roles and responsibilities of the emergency response team members.

Directions: Match the description with the appropriate team member. *Check your answers in Appendix B. (If you miss any items, review this section before continuing.)*

Role Description	Team Member
_____1. Secures the emergency area and controls crowds	a. Emergency Physician
_____2. Leads, advises, coordinates	b. Public Information Officer
_____3. Diagnoses, treats, and provides emergency medical care	c. Security Officer
_____4. Records and documents medical, hazardous materials, and radiological data	d. Team Coordinator
_____5. Releases accident information to the media	e. Technical Recorder

Preparing the Emergency Area (EA)

Upon notification of a hazardous material incident, the emergency response team prepares an area for patient reception. Special preparation techniques protect the attending staff, hospital facility, and equipment, while preventing the spread of contamination outside a designated decontamination area.

Hospitals and medical centers must determine where contaminated patients will be received. Separate ingress routes should be used for patients who are believed to be contaminated than those routes used for other patients. This may require the use of new traffic patterns for incoming vehicles. If different traffic patterns are used, traffic control and routing issues must be resolved through planning systems. Traffic patterns, both foot and vehicle, should be taken into account when designating response areas.

Procedures used in the handling of contaminated victims are similar to strict isolation precautions and to the protocol for "dirty" surgical cases.

Isolation

When contamination is suspected, strict isolation precautions are supplemented with contamination control techniques. This will prevent the spread of contaminants to the hospital environment and staff and simplify cleanup. Respiratory isolation may also be required for some hazardous materials that emit vapors, gases, or dust.

Designated Area for Patient Decontamination (appropriate for all hazards)

It may not be possible for a medical facility to have a dedicated decontamination area that meets basic criteria. In such cases, it may be necessary to improvise a decontamination area. This area should be large enough to hold one or more victims and the necessary medical personnel. Ventilation in the emergency area (EA) can be turned off by the hospital engineering department. Also, return air ducts can be closed or covered with filters. Although airborne contamination is unlikely, its removal from the air-conditioning system would be difficult.

Rolls of brown wrapping paper or butcher paper 3 to 4 feet wide can be unrolled to make a path from the ambulance entrance to the decontamination/treatment room. Ordinary sheet cloths or square absorbent pads (chux) can be used if paper is unavailable. The floor of the decontamination or treatment area should be covered the same way. This route and decontamination area should be marked off and labeled "Emergency Area: Do Not Enter." Whatever the floor covering, it should be taped securely to the floor. All seams should be sealed with tape to prevent tripping or spread of contaminants under the covering. The table on the following page summarizes these contamination control techniques.

All non-essential equipment and supplies in the room should be removed. This will simplify cleanup and decontamination. If a piece of equipment cannot be decontaminated or will be too expensive to decontaminate, it will need to be destroyed as contaminated waste. If it cannot be removed or is essential to patient care, it should be covered if possible. For example, monitor/defibrillator units can be covered with clear plastic sheeting and their screens still be seen. Equipment can be staged outside the room, and quickly brought into the room as the need arises. *Life support and other essential medical equipment and supplies should be available immediately and ready for use.*

Once all equipment and supplies in the room are removed or covered as appropriate, door handles and light switches can be covered by taping plastic sandwich bags or gloves over them to reduce contamination that might be spread by hand. A decontamination table can be prepared in a variety of ways. For example, a standard treatment table can be draped with a waterproof covering—a disposable surgical pack cover from the operating room is ideal. A burn table or specially designed decontamination tray can also be used. If desired, sheets can be rolled lengthwise and placed along the edges of a treatment table, then covered with plastic sheeting formed into a trough for fluid drainage.

Not all equipment can be decontaminated. The straps used on hospital carts cannot be decontaminated effectively and, after use, should be discarded. If wooden backboards are used, they can absorb contamination through scratches in the finish that allow the contamination to access the plywood base. Wooden backboards require either refinishing or replacement after use.

Control Zones

A control zone should be established for the decontamination area. A control line should be set up at the entrance to the EA to differentiate the controlled (contaminated or "hot") area from the noncontrolled (uncontaminated or "cold") area. Once the patient(s) is in the decontamination room, no person or equipment should leave the decontamination area until monitored at this control point for contamination, and decontaminated if needed. The personnel monitoring the control line should also function to limit entrance into the control area to essential personnel and equipment. Remember, if it enters, it is contaminated until proven otherwise, or decontaminated. A third zone (buffer or "warm" zone) can be set up between the contaminated and non-contaminated zone for added security.

Techniques for Contamination Control

The following table summarizes the basic steps that should be followed to control contamination.

Techniques for Contamination Control
1. Set up a controlled area large enough to hold the anticipated number of victims.
2. Prevent tracking of contaminants by covering floor areas.
3. Restrict access to the controlled area.
4. Monitor anyone or anything that leaves the controlled area.
5. Use strict isolation precautions, including protective clothing and bagging.
6. Use a buffer zone or secondary control line for added security.
7. Control waste by using large, plastic-lined containers for clothing, linens, dressings, etc.
8. Control ventilation.
9. Change instruments, outer glovers, drapes, etc. when they become contaminated.
10. Use waterproof materials to limit the spread of contaminated liquids; for example, waterproof aperture drapes.
11. Double bag all waste, contaminated or potentially contaminated objects.

Response Team Preparation (adequate for all hazards)

While the facility is being prepared, the response team members are required to dress in surgical clothing (scrub suit, gown, mask, cap, eye protection and gloves). Waterproof shoe covers should also be used. Pant and shirt cuffs should be taped over shoe covers and gloves; seams and zippers should be sealed with tape to prevent contaminants from getting under garments. A second pair of gloves should be placed over the taped ones. The second pair should be left untaped to allow for frequent glove changes as the outer gloves become contaminated. Other types of personal protective equipment will be required depending on the nature of the hazard.

Personal Protection Equipment (PPE)

The U.S. Environmental Protection Agency has identified four levels of protective ensembles, as described in the table below. The proper protective ensemble should be selected based upon levels of protection from chemical products required by medical staff. In most cases, disposable protective clothing, commonly made from coated Tyvek™ fabrics, is the choice. Common glove fabrics selected include neoprene, nitrile, and PVC materials.

Before using any protective equipment, the medical personnel must be trained in compliance with all applicable OSHA and state standards.

Levels of Personal Protection Equipment

Level A: This level of protection should be worn when the highest level of respiratory, skin, eye, and mucous membrane protection is needed. It consists of fully encapsulating, chemical resistant clothing and self-contained breathing apparatus.

Level B: This level of protection should be used when the highest level of respiratory protection is required, but a lesser level of skin and eye protection is sufficient.

Level C: This level of protection can be used when proper respiratory protection can be afforded by air-purifying, canister-equipped protective breathing devices. It provides the same level of skin protection as Level B, but a lower level of respiratory protection.

Level D: This protective ensemble consists primarily of a standard work uniform. It provides no respiratory protection and affords only minimal skin protection.

Exercise: What Supplies and Personal Protection Equipment Do Need To Be Prepared To Deal with Potential Hazardous Materials in Your Community?

Directions: Write down the items you would require to deal with the potential hazardous materials you identified in the exercise in Unit 2: *Identify Sources of Hazardous Materials in Your Community.*

 **Exercise: What's the Appropriate Method To Control the Spread of Hazardous Materials? (Unit 4)**

Purpose: To assess your understanding of the techniques used to control contamination.

Directions: Read each item and circle the most appropriate answer. *(You can check your answers* in *Appendix B. (If you missed any items, review this section before continuing.)*

1. A wounded patient walks into the reception area. The patient says he just provided assistance at a hazardous materials accident, but was injured when some kind of chemical exploded. What should you do?

   (a) Assume the patient is contaminated and immediately direct him or her back outside.
   (b) Fill out the patient's information and insurance forms.
   (c) Ask the patient to describe the type of accident at which he was providing assistance.
   (d) Tell the patient to wait for the next available doctor.

2. You have been notified that you will be receiving 10 patients who have been exposed to some type of corrosive. What should you do first?

   (a) Prepare the emergency area.
   (b) Contact the security officer to control the crowds.
   (c) Notify the public relations officer.
   (d) Call the hazardous materials hotline.

3. Which of the following will not help to prevent the spread of contamination in a hospital?

   (a) Failure to close the air ventilation ducts in the emergency area.
   (b) Establishing a control zone for the decontamination area.
   (c) Setting up a warm zone between the contaminated and non-contaminated area.
   (d) Using strict isolation precautions including protective clothing.

Hospital Emergency Department Management

Hospitals have rules and procedures that are used to quickly assess and treat patients. In routine situations, these procedures normally work very well. However, in dealing with hazardous materials incidents other variables can come into play that can throw these procedures into havoc. Therefore, you should be familiar with your facility's procedures for dealing with routine and nonroutine emergencies.

Patient Assessment and Triage

Triage refers to the process used to assess patients and determine the degree of urgency to treat the persons. For hazardous materials incidents, a triage area should be established near the treatment area. Priority should be given to medical and, when applicable, radiological problems. *Serious medical problems always have priority over other concerns, such as radiological exposure.* Therefore, in most cases, immediate assessment of the victim's airway, breathing, and circulation should be made and any necessary lifesaving measures performed. You should adhere to the "standard of care" rules dictated by your hospital.

Treatment of Radiation Contaminated Patients

Noncontaminated patients can be cared for like any other emergency cases. The victim of exposure without contamination does not pose a threat to anyone. Contaminated patients should be taken immediately to a decontamination area for treatment. Good judgment is essential in determining decontamination priorities. Since some chemicals are corrosive or toxic, medical attention might have to be directed first to those problems.

For example, a basic overview of the procedures for treating contaminated patients who have been exposed to radiation is shown below. Most of the procedures are similar for non-radiation exposed patients also, but you will not need to perform a radiological assessment. However, you may need to perform other assessments based on the information received from technical sources such as the Material Safety Data Sheets (MSDS) or the Agency for Toxic Substances and Disease Registry (ATSDR).

Example: Emergency Care of
Radiation Contaminated Patients

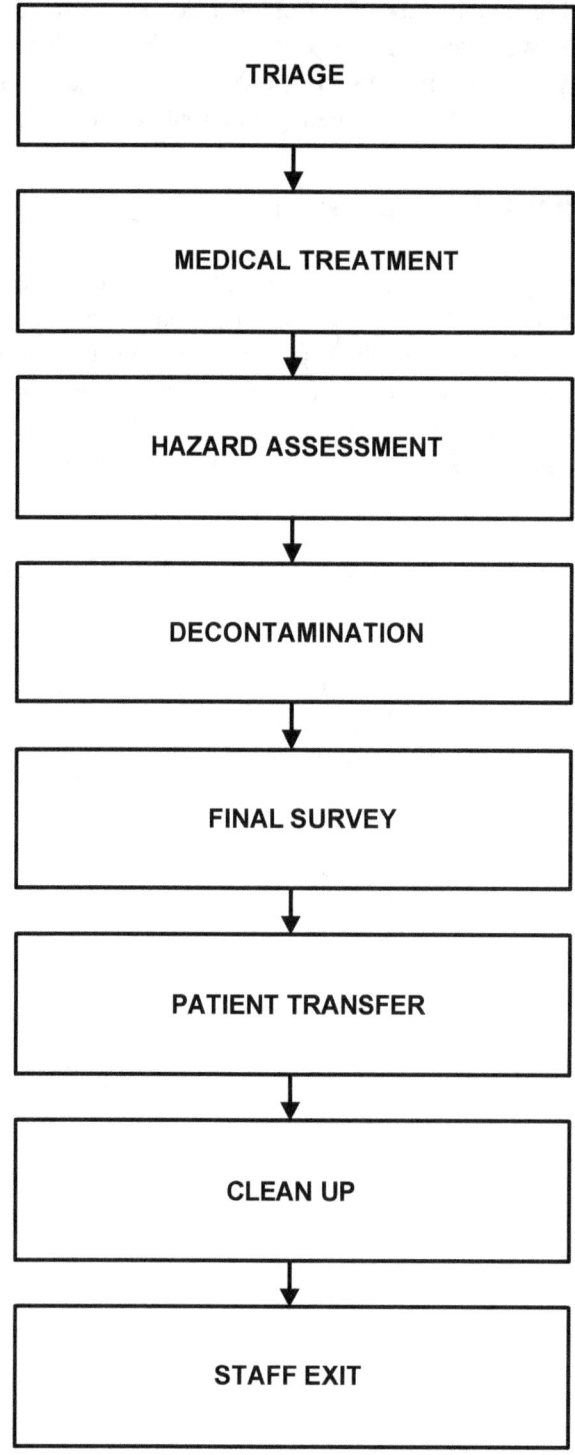

Laboratory Assessments

Types of Assessments

As with any situation, a complete and detailed medical, occupational, and accident history should be taken, and a physical examination completed. Certain clinical and laboratory analyses are also essential. A summary of some of the required samples appears in the table below.

Reasons for Assessments

These laboratory tests are performed to assess the biological effects, to identify abnormalities, to quantify radionuclide contamination if incident involves radioactive material, and to provide information useful in accident analysis. All samples collected should be labeled with date, time and exact site of collection such as "left nostril" in addition to patient name, number, etc.

Clinical and Laboratory Assessments		
SAMPLES NEEDED	**WHY**	**HOW**
In all cases of radiation injury: Complete blood count and differential STAT (follow with absolute lymphocyte counts every 6 hours for 48 hours when history indicates possibility of total-body irradiation)	For radiation exposures, to assess the radiation dose; initial counts establish a baseline, subsequent counts reflect the degree of injury	Choose a noncontaminated area for venipuncture; cover puncture site after collection
Routine urinalysis	To determine if kidneys are functioning normally and establish a baseline of urinary constituents; especially important if internal contamination is a possibility. Certain radioisotopes excrete or concentrate in urine.	Avoid contaminating specimen during collection; if necessary, give the patient plastic gloves to wear for collection of specimen; label specimen "Number 1," with date and time
When external contamination is suspected:		
Swabs from body orifices	To assess possibility of internal contamination	Use separate saline- or water-moistened swabs to wipe the inner aspect of each nostril, each ear, mouth, etc.

Swabs from wounds	To determine if wounds are contaminated	Use moist or dry swabs to sample secretions from each wound, or collect a few drops of secretion from each using a dropper or syringe. For wounds with visible debris, use applicator or long tweezers or forceps to transfer samples to specimen containers which are placed in lead storage containers
Skin wipes	To locate contaminated areas	Use filter paper, smear pads, or compresses to wipe sample areas 10 cm x 10 cm in size
When internal contamination with radioactive material is suspected:		
Urine: 24-hour specimen x 4 days	Body excreta may contain radionuclides if internal contamination has occurred	Use 24-hour urine collection container
Feces x 4 days	Body excreta may contain radionuclides if internal contamination has occurred	Save excreta in plastic containers in refrigerator or freezer
Vomitus	Body excreta may contain radionuclides if internal contamination has occurred	Save excreta in plastic containers in refrigerator or freezer
Sputum	To assess respiratory tract contamination if inhalation of contaminant was a possibility	Use 5-percent propylene-glycol aerosol to get a deep cough specimen for radiation victims
Serum creatinine, BUN	To assess kidney function if chelation is indicated	Clinical chemistry
Other samples needed:		
All irrigating fluids	Radiological and hazardous materials assessment	Save in sealed and labeled, glass- or plastic-lined containers

 **Exercise: Why Do I Need a Sample?**

Purpose: To assess your knowledge about why certain samples are required.

Directions: Match the correct sample with the reason it is required.
(Check your answers in Appendix B after you have finished. If you miss any, review this section again before proceeding.)

Sample	Reason Required
____1. Routine urinalysis	a. In accidents involving radiation, to assess the radiation dose and
____2. Swabs from wounds	b. To assess respiratory tract contamination if inhalation of contaminant was a possibility
____3. Sputum	c. To determine if wounds are contaminated
____4. Serum creatinine	d. To assess kidney function if chelation is indicated
____5. Complete Blood Count	e. To determine if kidneys are functioning normally

Job Aid

The following table lists some basic supplies needed to prepare the emergency department for the care of the contaminated patient.

Sample Supplies and Equipment Needed To Prepare the Emergency Department for the Care of the Contaminated Patient	
<ul><li>Brown wrapping paper</li><li>Masking tape</li><li>Rope</li><li>Caution Radiation Area signs</li><li>Decontamination table</li><li>5-gallon containers for wash water</li><li>Large waste containers lined with plastic bags</li><li>Cotton-tipped applicators</li><li>Various sizes of plastic bags</li><li>Small lead storage containers</li><li>Sterile saline</li><li>Sterile water</li><li>Sodium hypochlorite or household bleach</li><li>Providone iodine solution or other surgical soap</li><li>Soft scrub brushes</li><li>3-percent hydrogen peroxide solution</li></ul>	<ul><li>Shampoo</li><li>Emergency medical supplies and equipment (such as suction, oxygen, airways intubation, IV solutions, etc.)</li><li>Scrub suits</li><li>Gowns</li><li>Surgical hoods</li><li>Masks</li><li>Surgical gloves of various sizes</li><li>Waterproof shoe covers</li><li>Film badges</li><li>Dosimeters and/or survey meters</li><li>Rubber or plastic aprons</li><li>Batteries</li><li>Wax or felt tip pens</li><li>Radioactive labels</li><li>Sheets, blankets, towels, patient gowns</li></ul>

Introduction to Decontamination

Proper decontamination is important in responding to hazardous materials incidents. Quick actions can prevent the spread of contamination, minimize vapor exposures and help save lives.

Purpose of Decontamination

Decontamination is performed for the following reasons:

- To reduce skin damage and the absorption factor of the contaminant through the skin

- To minimize the chance of inhalation or ingestion

- To protect the health of medical care providers

- To control the spread of contamination to equipment and facilities

- To determine damage done by the hazardous material

Mechanisms for Decontamination

There are seven common mechanisms for performing **gross** and **secondary decontamination**: emulsification, chemical reaction, disinfection, dilution, absorption, removal and disposal.

Gross decontamination is the removal or chemical alteration of the majority of the contaminant. It must be assumed that some residual contamination will remain on the host. This residual contamination can produce cross-contamination.

Secondary decontamination is the removal or alteration of most of the residual product contamination. It provides a more thorough decontamination than the gross effort. However, some contaminant may still remain.

Mechanisms for Decontamination

Emulsification. This is the production of a suspension of ordinarily immiscible/insoluble materials, using an emulsifying agent such as a surfactant, soap, or detergent. Emulsification is most often used for nonpolar liquids (i.e., gasoline, or toluene) and insoluble solids (i.e., iodine crystals).

Chemical Reaction or Degradation. This is a process that neutralizes, degrades, or otherwise chemically alters the contaminant. Normally, a chemical reaction does not assure that all hazards have been eliminated, and the reactions can be both difficult and dangerous to perform. It is, therefore, not recommended for use on living tissue.

Disinfection. This process removes the biological (etiologic) contamination hazards as the disinfectant destroys microorganisms and their toxins. It is the method of choice for many biohazards. Bleach and hydrogen peroxide are commonly used products.

Dilution. This process simply reduces the concentration of the contaminant. It is most commonly used for those substances that are miscible/soluble. Huge quantities of solvent may be required to dilute even small volumes of some solute contaminants. You must exercise caution with products that are water reactive because chemical or thermal burns on the patient may occur in some cases. *Know the product before you act.* This method may not be effective with nonwater-soluble materials that may require other agents.

Absorption. This is the penetration of a liquid or gas into another substance. A classic example of this process is when a sponge absorbs water. This method has no practical role in the decontamination of victims. This is generally used for large-scale removal of contaminants from the environment, such as from the surface of water.

Removal. This is the physical process of removing contaminants by pressure or vacuum. Most efforts involve the use of water, though some solids can be removed with brushes and wipes, and even air can be used. You must take special precautions to avoid inhaling the airborne dusts and vapors while performing mechanical removal.

Disposal. This process is the aseptic removal of a contaminated object (personal protective equipment, other equipment, etc.) from a host, after which the object is directly disposed. The host object is never really decontaminated. It is not the method of choice in dealing with patients, but is likely to be used in dealing with the contaminated clothing of victims and emergency workers.

Exercise: What Do You Know About Mechanisms for Decontamination?

Purpose: To assess your knowledge of ways to perform gross and secondary decontamination.

Directions: Match the descriptions of decontamination mechanisms with the appropriate terms. *(Check your answers in Appendix B. If you miss any items, review this section before proceeding.)*

Description	Term
____ 1. Process that neutralizes, degrades, or otherwise chemically alters the contaminant.	a. Absorption
____ 2. Destroys microorganisms and their toxins.	b. Dilution
____ 3. Penetration of liquid or gas into another substance.	c. Disposal
____ 4. Used more often to deal with contaminated clothing.	d. Degradation
____ 5. Reduces the concentration of the contaminant.	e. Disinfection

Methods for Decontamination

There are two basic methods of decontamination: dry and wet. Though a contaminant may or may not be liquid, dry methods are an effective means of decontamination. These include the mechanisms of disposal and absorption, which use no liquids. Equipment may be vacuumed, or disposable outer suit coverings may be worn, providing what is known as double enveloping.

Nonwater-Based Methods

Nonwater-based solutions, like those used for degradation operations, are contaminant-specific. In general, they are used for equipment only, because they are hydrocarbon and halogenated hydrocarbon compounds.

Wet Methods

Wet methods, though they may have some dry operational steps, principally involve the use of liquids. Wet methods are used in emulsification and dilution operations. The wet solutions may be either water-based or nonwater-based. The water-based solutions may function as emulsifiers, neutralizers, degraders, or disinfectants.

Emulsifiers have a "loosening" effect on the bonding nature of a contaminant. Laundry detergent, preferably liquid, is an example of an emulsifying agent. Trisodium phosphate is another example, but it is deemed too harsh because of its capacity to destroy the protective qualities of PPE. In itself it is a potential hazard to the environment.

Neutralizers are used to negate the destructive forces of either an acid or a base (caustic or alkaline). Sodium carbonate or the like might be used to neutralize an acid. Large amounts of heat may be generated.

Degradation Solutions may be quite complex, as they often must be contaminant-specific. This means that general answers cannot be offered. Specific solutions to a given problem may require the use of chemical and/or biological agents. In one instance, chemical oxidation or reduction may solve a problem. In another case, enzymes or microbial agents may be necessary.

Disinfection Procedures, such as the use of chlorine bleach, are also a means of decontamination.

The decontamination mechanisms of disinfection, chemical reaction, and removal all may occur through either a wet or dry method. The specific procedure for decontamination will vary according to the chemical to which the individual was exposed. Certain items—for example, leather and some plastic and rubber materials—absorb toxic substances so easily that they cannot be completely decontaminated; these items must be discarded or disposed of.

Decontamination Process

In all cases, it is important to attend to lifesaving needs before beginning decontamination. In most instances, contaminated wounds and orifices are decontaminated first, followed by areas of highest contamination levels on intact skin. Decontamination should begin with the least aggressive method and progress to more aggressive ones. You will learn more about decontamination in the classroom course.

The decontamination process consists of the following steps:

Step 1—Remove gross decontamination from the patient.
Step 2—Treat patient's medical needs.
Step 3—Fully clean the patient.
Step 4—Decontaminate staff after treatment is completed.
Step 5—Decontaminate facility.

Hazardous Materials Resources

There are numerous resources available to help hospital personnel deal with hazardous materials incidents. Some of the more important resources are described below.

Written Information and Publicly Available On-line Database Sources

Material Safety Data Sheet (MSDS). Chemical manufacturers and importers must develop a Material Safety Data Sheet (MSDS) for each hazardous chemical they produce or import. Each MSDS includes information regarding the specific chemical identity of the hazardous chemical(s) involved and the common names. In addition, it provides:

- information on the physical and chemical characteristics of the hazardous chemical;
- known acute and chronic health effects and related health information;
- exposure limits;
- whether the chemical is considered a carcinogen by the National Toxicology Program, IARC, or OSHA;
- precautionary measures;
- emergency and first aid procedures; and
- the identification of the organization responsible for preparing the sheet.

These MSDS sheets are also available in computerized formats and through on-line databases. *Check to see if your facility has copies of or access to the MSDS.*

The Emergency Response Guidebook for Selected Hazardous Materials, U.S. Department of Transportation. This is a good resource to help identify hazardous materials. However, it does not provide information on treatment for people exposed to the hazardous materials. This book is more useful for field personnel than for hospital staff.

Recognition and Management of Pesticide Poisoning by the Environmental Protection Agency. This document concentrates on pesticide poisonings and provides good information on decontamination activities and treatment protocols.

Chemical Hazards Information Response System (CHRIS), produced by the U.S. Coast Guard, provides information for emergency response during transport of hazardous chemicals. Contains information on labeling, physical and chemical properties, fire hazards, chemical reactivity, water pollution, and hazard classifications for more than 1,016 substances.

TOXNET system is a computer database operated by the National Library of Medicine. Your facility can preregister with TOXNET for system access. TOXNET printouts provide extensive information on chemical substances. The Hazardous Substance Database, part of the TOXNET system, includes a POISINDEX® protocol for patient care and treatment.

Sources of Assistance

Joint Commission on Accreditation of Healthcare Organizations (JCAHO) establishes standards for hospital accreditation. Some of these standards are related to minimum standards for responding to hazardous materials events and for identifying and controlling hazardous materials in the facility.

Occupational Safety and Health Administration (OSHA) provides information on interpreting the OSHA requirements and on meeting the applicable standards.

National Institute for Occupational Safety and Health (NIOSH) provides printed material related to employee safety and health in the workplace.

The Chemical Emergency Transportation Center (CHEMTREC) is a public service operated by the Chemical Manufacturers Association. CHEMTREC can provide valuable assistance in identifying chemical substances and can provide telephone conference connections with the manufacturer or representatives of the materials in question. Many chemical manufacturers have toxicologists who can be reached through the CHEMTREC network. There is no charge for the services of this organization.

Agency for Toxic Substances and Disease Registry (ATSDR) operates a telephone hotline for information on chemical exposures. This telephone service can provide medical personnel with valuable information on treatment protocols, therapies, decontamination methods, and other related topics. There is no charge for their services.

Local or Regional Poison Control Centers can provide information on the treatment and toxicity of many substances. They also usually have a toxicologist available for consultation on a 24-hour basis.

There are numerous other sources that you can consult, such as your local emergency management office and local colleges and universities.

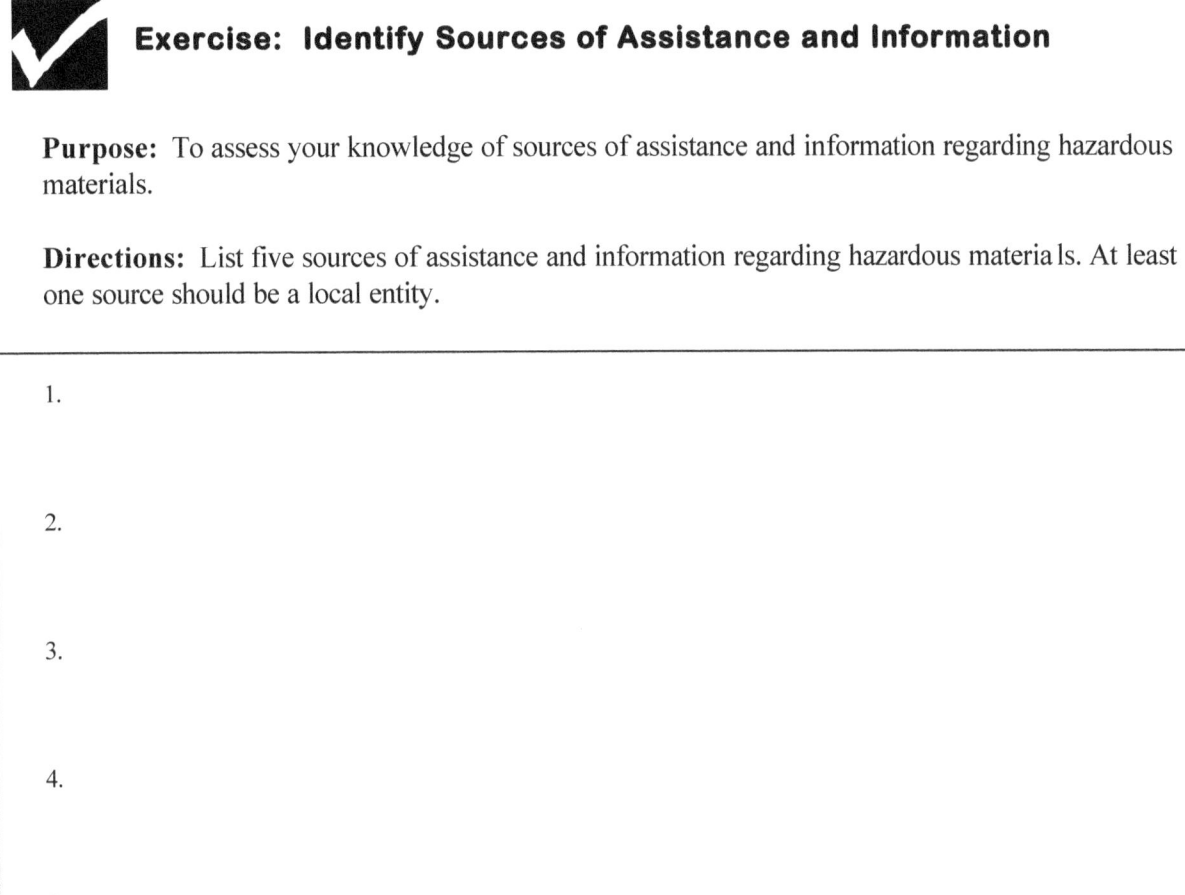

Exercise: Identify Sources of Assistance and Information

Purpose: To assess your knowledge of sources of assistance and information regarding hazardous materials.

Directions: List five sources of assistance and information regarding hazardous materials. At least one source should be a local entity.

1.

2.

3.

4.

5.

 **References**

FEMA, EPA, DOT. 1993. *Hazardous Materials Workshop for Hospital Staff.* Emmitsburg, MD.

FEMA, USFA, NFA. 1995. *Basic Life Support and Hazardous Materials Response.* Emmitsburg, MD.

FEMA, EMI. 1984. *Hospital Emergency Department Management of Radiation Accidents.* Emmitsburg, MD (out of print).

UNIT 4: POST-TEST

Directions: Answer each of the questions below.

(*Check your answers in Appendix B. If you missed any items, you should review this unit before proceeding.*)

1. When notified of a hazardous materials incident and the possible transport of patients, what should you do?

    a) Get accurate and complete information from the person reporting the incident.
    b) Call the local emergency management office to coordinate patient treatment.
    c) Notify the American Red Cross.
    d) Wait until the patients arrive before taking any action.

2. When a substance actually touches a body or thing, it is called

    a) Cross contamination
    b) Decontamination
    c) Direct or primary contamination
    d) Contaminated

3. Which of the following statements is not a characteristic of the emergency response team (ERT)?

    a) The composition of the ERT may vary from facility to facility.
    b) The hospital ERT must coordinate its efforts with field emergency response teams and other external agencies.
    c) The composition of the team, and the numbers of people needed will vary according to the magnitude of the situation.
    d) The ERT consists of a limited number of people, usually the triage officer, nurse, and emergency physician.

4. It is important to prepare an emergency area when dealing with hazardous materials incidents because:

    a) Special preparation techniques protect the attending staff, hospital facility, and equipment while preventing the spread of contamination.
    b) It will be easier for family members to see the patient.
    c) Doctors and nurses prefer to work in separate areas.
    d) It allows for continuous traffic flow and visitor movement within the area.

UNIT 4: POST-TEST

5. Protocol for "dirty" surgical cases is similar to the techniques applied in:

   a) Treating ill patients
   b) Isolation of contaminated patients
   c) Diagnosing wounded patients
   d) Triage

6. To prepare a room for decontamination, you should:

   a) Turn off the ventilation system.
   b) Cover the movable equipment.
   c) Set up an open access area.
   d) Avoid using control lines or control zones.

7. Personal protection equipment should only be used when

   a) Personnel have been trained in the OSHA requirements regarding its use
   b) Poisonous vapors are present
   c) Instructed to do so by the ERT coordinator
   d) You perceive a danger

8. In dealing with hazardous materials incidents during patient assessment and triage

   a) You should follow routine procedures in all situations.
   b) You should care for noncontaminated patients like any other emergency case.
   c) You should take all patients to a decontamination area.
   d) You should wait until you have details on the nature of the hazard before doing anything.

9. Which of the following is *not* a reason you perform radiological and clinical laboratory assessments:

   a) To assess the biological effects
   b) To identify abnormalities
   c) To quantify radionuclide contamination, if exposed to radiation
   d) To aid in the detection of the hazard

10. When you perform gross decontamination, you

   a) Remove or alter chemically the majority of the contaminant
   b) Remove all traces of the contaminant
   c) Ensure that cross contamination does not occur
   d) Create potential hazards

UNIT 5:

Introduction to Radiation
Health Effects of Radiation

Understanding Radiation—Getting the Essential Concepts

You have just gained a basic awareness of how hazardous materials incidents can affect your involvement and hospitals' involvement in responding to such incidents. As you learned, radioactive materials are just one type of hazardous material. However, there are some basic concepts you need to understand about radiation and radioactive materials. These basic concepts will provide a solid foundation for taking additional course work in responding to radiation-related hazardous events and will prepare you for the classroom course on managing radiation accidents.

Overview

This unit identifies sources of radiation and presents data on the frequency of radiation accidents. It describes the types of radiation injuries and provides an overview of radiation physics. This unit also describes how to measure radioactivity and the types of instruments used to measure it, defines some basic radiation protection principles, and presents the recommended radiation exposure limits. It also covers basic biophysical and biological effects of ionizing radiation, to provide a foundation for understanding the clinical aspects of radiation injuries.

Objectives

At the end of this unit, you will be able to:

1. Identify sources of radiation.

2. State the prevalence of radiation accidents.

3. Identify types of radiation injuries and differentiate among them.

4. Define ionizing radiation.

5. Explain the differences among the various types of ionizing radiation in terms of penetrating power and effects on living tissue.

6. Define the terms curie, rem, rad, roentgen, and their SI units.

7. State four radiation protection principles and explain their use in reducing radiation exposure.

8. State the use and limitations of the survey meters and dosimeters.

9. Describe methods of contamination.

10. Establish patient management priorities.

11. List practical ways of reducing radiation exposure.

12. Define the effect chemicals may have on a radiation-contaminated patient.

13. Describe the dose-response relationship and its clinical effects.

14. Describe the routes by which any hazardous substance may enter the body.

15. Describe the organ systems that may be affected in the contaminated or exposed patient.

16. Distinguish between stages of acute radiation syndrome.

17. State the nature of radiological and chemical hazards.

18. Summarize the toxic effects of some radioisotopes.

Pretest

If you think you have the requisite skills and knowledge for this topic area, take the pretest on the next page. If you score 85 percent or higher, you can skip this unit. However, this unit is recommended because it will prepare you for the classroom course that deals primarily with managing radiation incidents.

UNIT 5: PRETEST

Directions: Answer each question. Each answer counts 20 points. After you have completed the test, check your answers in Appendix B.

1. Can incorporation occur without contamination? Explain your answer.

2. What are the three most common types of ionizing radiation?

3. What is the most penetrating type of ionizing radiation?

4. List two units of quantity of measuring radioactivity.

5. List three elements of radiation protection.

Introduction to Radiation Accidents

Sources of Radioactive Materials

Radiation comes from outer space, the ground, and even from within our own bodies. Radiation is all around us and has been present since the birth of this planet. Radiation occurs naturally and in man-made sources. The table below shows some other sources of radiation.

Sources of Radioactive Materials	
Radiation Source	**Relative Dose (Millirem)**
Gastrointestinal series (upper and lower)	1,400 millirem
Radon in average household in the U.S.	200 millirem annually
Living in Denver	81 millirem annually
X-rays and nuclear medicine	50 millirem annually
Natural radioactivity in the body	39 millirem annually
Living in Chicago	34 millirem annually
Cosmic radiation	31 millirem annually
Mammogram	30 millirem
Living at sea level	28 millirem annually
Consumer products (such as drinking water)	11 millirem annually
Chest x-ray	10 millirem
Living near a nuclear power station	less than 1 millirem annually

Radiation used in medicine is the largest source of man-made radiation to which we are exposed. Most of our exposure is to diagnostic x-rays—Americans receive 200 million x-rays every year. Radiation is also used in cancer treatments. One-third of all successful cancer treatments involve radiation.

Nuclear power plants use radioactive materials (uranium or plutonium) to generate electricity, and any activity that uses radioactive materials generates radioactive waste. Mining, nuclear power, defense, nuclear medicine and scientific research all produce radioactive waste that must be disposed of properly.

Frequencies and Prevalence of Radiation Accidents

Radiation accidents do occur, though their number and frequency vary. Fortunately, few radiation accidents pose life-threatening hazards because of the many control procedures and mechanisms that are in place. However, when these controls fail, the results can be devastating and often fatal.

Number of Accidents, Exposures, and Fatalities

Radiation accidents can occur at biological firms, medical offices, hospitals, industrial labs, nuclear power plants, military installations and transportation routes (land, sea, air).

Medical Misadministrations

The Nuclear Regulatory Commission and Agreement States reported the following medical misadministration related incidents for radiation during January 1, 1994 through September 30, 1995. As shown in the table below, the majority of the misadministrations involved brachytherapy treatment; sodium iodide procedures were the second highest. Misadministrations involving dose variances during brachytherapy and sodium iodide treatments most often result in an overdose rather than an underdose. Teletherapy and gamma stereotactic radiosurgery were exclusively overdoses.

These problems occurred for the following reasons: communication problems due to misunderstanding the physician's request, not following the quality management plan, and not properly documenting changes to the treatment plan. Human error problems included incorrect calculation of the treatment plan and errors in operating the equipment.

Medical Misadministrations Reported by NRC (1994-1995)	
Procedure	Number
Diagnostic radiopharmaceutical	1
Sodium iodide radiopharmaceutical	14
Brachytherapy	42
Teletherapy	12
Gamma Stereotactic Radiosurgery	1
TOTAL	69
Source: Annual Report, 1994-FY 95, Nuclear Materials, Office for Analysis and Evaluation of Operational Data, U.S. Nuclear Regulatory Commission	

Radiation Exposures

Over 80 percent of our exposure to radiation comes from natural sources. Fifty-five percent of our exposure to natural sources of radiation usually comes from radon. Radon is a colorless, tasteless, and odorless gas that comes from the decay of uranium found in nearly all soils. Our own bodies, which contain and concentrate the radioactive element potassium, account for 11 percent of our total exposure. Another three percent of our exposure to radiation comes from consumer products. The average annual radiation exposure for persons living in the United States is 360 millirem.

There were some radiation overexposures reported also, as listed in the table below.

Radiation Overexposures Reported by NRC (1994-1995)	
Type of Licensee	**Number of Individuals**
Medical/Academic	4
Research/Commercial	37
Industrial Radiography	16
TOTAL	**57**
Source: Annual Report, 1994-FY 95, Nuclear Materials, Office for Analysis and Evaluation of Operational Data, U.S. Nuclear Regulatory Commission	

The primary causes of medical/academic and research/commercial overexposures included failure to ensure that adequate dosimetry was issued and monitored, failure to wear adequate protective clothing in areas containing discrete radioactive particles, and failure to follow procedures. The primary causes of industrial radiography exposure were failure to conduct the required radiation surveys, failure to set up or monitor radiation boundaries, failure to follow established emergency procedures, and lack of adequate supervision of assistants.

Radioactive Alerts

NRC-licensed nuclear materials facilities reported the following alerts in 1994 and 1995.

Radioactive Alerts Reported by NRC (1994-1995)		
Facility	**Description**	**Duration**
Westinghouse (Fuel Facility)	Uranium hexafluoride release	2 hours, 35 minutes
Allied-Signal (Fuel Facility)	Leak of uranium hexafluoride from a loose cylinder connection into the feed material building	50 minutes
Babcock & Wilcox (Fuel Facility)	Plant evacuation due to a nitric acid spill	3 hours, 5 minutes
Source: Annual Report, 1994-FY 95, Nuclear Materials, Office for Analysis and Evaluation of Operational Data, U.S. Nuclear Regulatory Commission		

Radiation Accidents Requiring Hospital Emergency Services

The following are representative examples of radiation accidents that require hospital emergency services.

1. Goiania, Brazil
    In 1985, a private radiotherapy clinic moved to a new location and abandoned a Cs-137 radiotherapy unit. Two people found the abandoned unit and took it home, not knowing what it was but believing that it had some scrap value. While attempting to dismantle it, they broke open the source capsule, releasing the Cs-137 that was in the form of a soluble chloride salt, heavily contaminating the premises. The unit with the ruptured capsule was sold to a junkyard owner for scrap. He noticed that the capsule glowed blue in the dark, and had people come and see this and distributed pieces of the Cs-137 salt to friends and family members. Several people became ill with gastrointestinal symptoms, but did not connect it to the source. One person did make the connection, and took the capsule to the public health department. Twenty people were identified as needing hospital treatment; four died within 4 weeks of the exposure, and their doses were estimated from 4.5 to 6 Gy. One hundred twelve thousand people were monitored for contamination, and 249 were found to be contaminated externally and/or internally—some quite heavily. In addition, the environment was heavily contaminated and required extensive decontamination, producing more than 275 truckloads of waste estimated to contain 1,200 Ci of Cs-137.

2. Springfield, Massachusetts
    On December 16, 1991, a truck carrying new fuel from Wilmington, North Carolina to Yankee Nuclear Power Station in Vernon, Vermont, was involved in an accident when it collided with a car traveling in the wrong direction. The truck and radioactive material were engulfed in flames. The truck drivers were transported to the hospital by ambulance unattended due to concerns over contamination. The hospital was informed enroute of the possibility of contamination with radioactive material, but did not receive detailed information until about one-half hour after arrival. The patients were taken to the decontamination room, were examined and found to be uncontaminated, and were treated for minor injuries and released. The driver of the car was also transported, found to be uncontaminated, treated and released. The fire was allowed to burn itself out. The fuel containers did not breach, and no environmental contamination was found.

Do you know what type of radiation accidents your facility has responded to in the last year?

Types of Radiation Injuries

There are three types of radiation injuries: external irradiation, contamination, and incorporation.

External Irradiation occurs when all or part of the body is exposed to penetrating radiation from an external source. A similar thing occurs during an ordinary chest X-ray. *A person who has been exposed to radiation from an external source, but has not been contaminated by the radioactive material, is NOT radioactive and presents no danger to caregivers.*

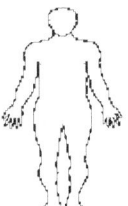

Whole Body (total) exposure occurs when the entire body is irradiated more or less uniformly from an external source. In addition, when a radioactive material is uniformly distributed throughout the body tissues rather than being concentrated in certain organs, the irradiation can be considered whole-body exposure as well as the patient being contaminated.

Local exposure occurs when a radioactive material is concentrated in certain organs or body parts, or when a local portion of the body is irradiated, such as a hand.

External Contamination means that radioactive materials in the form of gases, liquids or solids are released into the environment and contaminate people externally, such as on skin and clothing. This type of contamination is the easiest to remove.

Internal Contamination refers to radioactive materials being taken up into the body, and being contained in the gut, lungs and blood or extracellular fluids. This requires the radioactive materials to enter through a 'portal of entry' such as the mouth, nose, eyes, wounds or other skin breaks. The vagina and anus can also serve as portals of entry if the mucosa becomes contaminated. Intact skin forms a good barrier to most forms of radioactive materials.

Incorporation refers to the uptake of radioactive materials by body cells, tissues and target organs such as bone, liver, thyroid or kidney. Radioactive materials are distributed throughout the body based on their chemical properties. Incorporation cannot occur unless contamination has occurred. Incorporation can occur rapidly, within as little as an hour or less. This is the most difficult type of contamination to remove. Radioisotopes have chemical properties identical to their stable counterparts. For example, a thyroid cell will take up radioactive I-131 and use it to make thyroid hormone just as it would stable I-127. The cell will be unable to tell the difference until the I-131 decays to Xe-131, emitting a beta particle and gamma radiation.

Exercise: Identifying Types of Radiation Injuries

Purpose: To assess your understanding of the types of radiation injuries.

Directions: Answer each question. You can check your answers in Appendix B. If you missed any, review this section before continuing.

1. Mary had a series of x-rays taken during her visit to the emergency room. What type of radiation exposure did she receive?

2. Jim spilled a radioactive material on his skin. Is Jim exposed, contaminated or both?

3. Three school children accidentally picked up an unbroken, sealed container that had dropped off a truck that was carrying radioactive materials. Is it possible that they could experience incorporation? Why or why not?

4. Will these children be radioactive or dangerous to care for?

Radiation Physics

A fundamental knowledge of atomic structure and matter is helpful in understanding radioactivity.

Atomic Structure

Elements are substances that cannot be broken down into simpler substances by any chemical means. There are 105 known elements, each with specific characteristics. The atom is the simplest unit into which an element can be divided and still retain the specific properties of the original element. Molecules are combinations of two or more atoms. Molecules can be as small as 2 atoms such as O_2 or as large as proteins that may contain thousands of atoms. Each element is identified by a one- or two-letter symbol, such as O for oxygen, He for helium, Pb for lead, etc.

Atoms

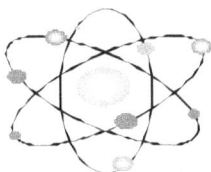

An **atom** is composed of a central nucleus, containing most of its mass, and electrons orbiting in shells around the nucleus. The nucleus consists of a number of fundamental particles, including protons and neutrons. The number of protons determines the type of atom or the element (hydrogen, oxygen, etc.) and also equals the atomic number. Some atoms are stable while others are unstable. Unstable atoms attempt to stabilize by emitting energy and particles from their nuclei in the form of ionizing radiation. Atoms that emit ionizing radiation are radioactive. Electrons have a negative electrical charge, protons have a positive charge, and neutrons carry no charge.

Neutrons

The neutron is an uncharged particle having a mass similar to that of a proton, approximately equal to the masses of a proton and an electron. They interact directly with atomic nuclei. Because of their mass and energy, neutrons can cause severe disruptions in atomic structure. (In addition, they have the ability to convert stable isotopes to radioisotopes.) Neutron radiation is significant mainly in nuclear fuel, weapons and research types of facilities.

Ions

Atoms are electrically neutral when the number of negatively charged electrons orbiting the nucleus equals the number of positively charged protons within the nucleus. When the number of electrons is greater than or less than the number of protons in the nucleus, the atoms are not electrically neutral and carry a net negative or positive charge, respectively. At this point they are called **ions** and tend to combine with other ions of opposite net charge to form a neutral molecule.

Ionizing Radiation

Ionizing radiation is radiation that can produce charged particles (ions) in any material it strikes. These charged particles can cause damage to molecules, cells, or tissues. The three most common types of ionizing radiation are alpha particles, beta particles, and gamma rays.

Radiation Energy. Each type of radiation can be emitted with various levels of energy, measured in eV (electron volts). Due to the magnitude of the numbers, energies are usually expressed in KeV (thousands) and MeV (millions).The type of radiation and its energy are unique to the type of radioactive material and can be used to identify it.

Alpha (α) Particles

Alpha particles are positively charged particles consisting of two protons and two neutrons all strongly bound together by nuclear forces. They are the heaviest of the radioactive particle s. Alpha particles have a mass about 7000 times the mass of electrons and are ejected from the nuclei of radioactive atoms with one or several characteristic and discrete energies. Alpha particles are the least penetrating of the three types of ionizing radiation. They do not penetrate the dead layer of skin and can be stopped by a piece of paper or clothing. They are, however, not a "safe" type of radiation. They are energetic particles that transfer their energy over a short distance, doing a great deal of damage. A health hazard may occur when alpha-emitting materials are inhaled or swallowed, or enter the body through a wound, depositing themselves near or in cells where the energetic alpha particles will do extensive damage when released. Thus, alpha particles are essentially an internal hazard only.

Beta (β) Particles

Beta particles are high-speed, charged particles with a moderate penetrating power. These particles have the characteristics of electrons, and are negatively charged. Beta particles can travel several hundred times the distance of alpha particles in the air and can penetrate into skin and cause severe skin burns. They require fairly thin (a few millimeters) shielding such as thin metal, wallboard or heavy clothing to stop them. Thus, beta particles can be an external and an internal hazard because they can injure from both the outside and inside of the body.

Gamma (γ) Rays

Gamma rays are electromagnetic radiation emitted from the nucleus of a radioactive atom. Gamma rays are the most penetrating type of radiation and can travel many meters to miles in air and deeply into tissue, doing damage to deep organs. Because gamma rays can travel through the body, they are sometimes referred to as "penetrating radiation." Like emitters of beta particles, gamma rays constitute an internal and an external hazard.

Neutrons

The neutron is an uncharged particle having a mass similar to that of a proton, approximately equal to the masses of a proton and an electron. They interact directly with atomic nuclei. Because of their mass and energy, neutrons can cause severe disruptions in atomic structure. (In addition, they have the ability to convert stable isotopes to radioisotopes.) Neutron radiation is significant mainly in nuclear fuel, weapons and research types of facilities.

Isotopes and Nuclides

Isotopes are forms of the same element that differ by the number of neutrons in the nucleus. Since they are the same element, they have the same number of protons, and thus the same atomic number. Since the number of neutrons is different, the atomic mass number (number of protons + neutrons) will be different, and is how the isotope is identified. For example, hydrogen has three isotopes, with one, two, and three atomic mass units (one proton each, plus 0, 1 and 2 neutrons, respectively). H-1 is 'normal' hydrogen; H-2 and H-3 are commonly called deuterium and tritium, respectively. The first two of these are stable (nonradioactive), but tritium is a radioactive isotope. Isotopes are identified by their symbol and mass number, as in H-2, etc. They can also be written as hydrogen-2, or ^{2}H. The atomic number may also be included as a subscript ^{2}H$_\square$.

The central core of an atom is the **nucleus** and contains nearly all of the atom's mass. Different types of nuclei are called **nuclides**. For example, the nucleus of an I-131 atom is called its nuclide. In common use, isotope and nuclide can be used interchangeably. A nuclide is characterized by its mass number as well as its atomic number.

The terms "radioisotope" and "radionuclide" merely denote the radioactive forms.

Radioactive Decay

Radioactive decay is a process whereby an unstable nucleus attempts to stabilize through the emission of energetic particles (alpha, beta, neutron) and/or pure energy (gamma). Emission of an alpha particle results in the loss of 2 neutrons and 2 protons. This results in a new element being produced because these particles are being ejected from the nucleus. These new atoms are called "daughters." Sometimes they are successful in producing a stable atom. Sometimes, however, several decays are needed to produce a stable daughter, as in the decay of Uranium (U) that will undergo over 10 decays before it finally becomes stable lead (Pb). Every decay produces a new daughter. The following diagram illustrates the penetrating power of the different types of radiation.

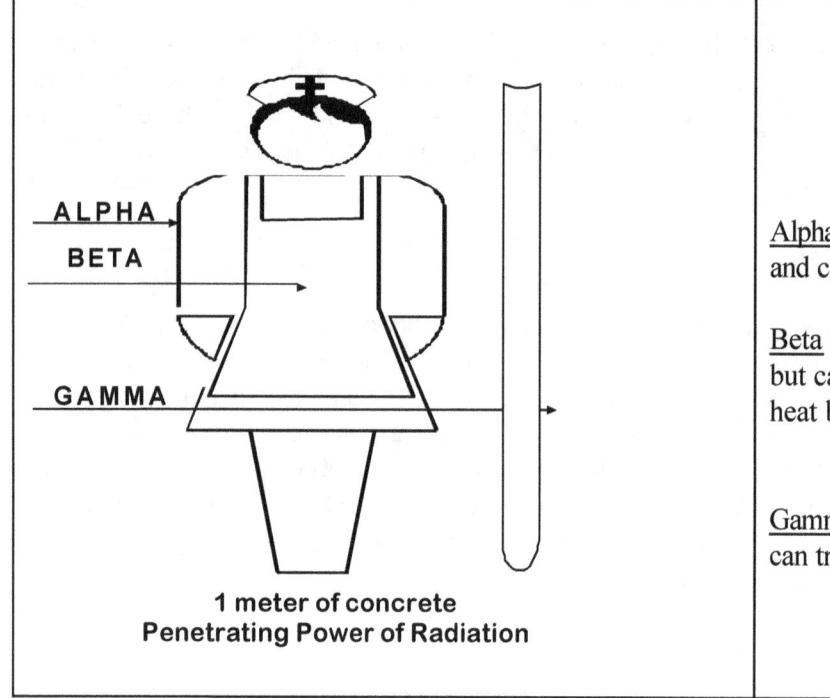

ALPHA

BETA

GAMMA

1 meter of concrete
Penetrating Power of Radiation

Alpha can be stopped by your skin and clothing.

Beta can be stopped by your clothing but can penetrate your skin and cause heat burns.

Gamma is the most penetrating and can travel through the body.

Measuring Radioactivity

When dealing with radiation, it is important to know how much radiation is present and the extent of exposure over a period of time. Radioactivity is measured in units of quantity, as described below.

Units of Quantity (Amount) of Radioactive Material

Different radioactive materials emit very different amounts of radiation. Thus, conventional units of mass or weight such as the kilogram or pound do not relate to the amount of radiation being emitted from a sample of radioactive material and are not effective units to measure quantity. The **curie (Ci)** measures the amount of radioactive material based on the amount of radiation emitted and allows better comparison of different types of radioactive materials. One curie of radioactive material is defined as the amount of radioactive material undergoing 37 billion decays per second, regardless of it's mass.

The international system of units is based on the meter (length), kilogram (mass), and the liter (volume), and is known as **Systems International (SI)**. The SI unit corresponding to the curie is the SI unit of the Becquerel (Bq), and is defined as an amount of radioactive material undergoing 1 decay per second.
1 Ci = 37 GBq

Millicurie (mCi). One thousandth of a curie.

Microcurie (μCi.). One millionth of a curie.

Megabecquerel (MBq). One million Bq.

Gigabecquerel(GBq) One billion Bq.

Units of Absorbed Dose

Dose means the total amount of radiation or energy absorbed. **Absorbed Dose** is the energy imparted to matter by ionizing radiation per unit mass of irradiated material. The **total dose** = dose rate x exposure time. For example, 25 R/hr (dose rate) x 1/2 hour (exposure time) = 12.5 R (total dose).

Exposure (Dose) Rate

The exposure (dose) rate is the amount of radiation exposure per unit of time, usually per hour. The exposure rate is generally expressed in roentgens per hour or in milliroentgens per hour on most of the instruments in common use.

Radiation Absorbed Dose (Rad). Rad is a measure of the energy deposited in matter by ionizing radiation or, in other words, an indication of how much immediate damage radiation causes to matter. The SI Unit is the **Gray (Gy)**. 1 Rad = 0.01 Gy, or 100 Rad = 1 Gy.

Units of Exposure

Roentgen (R). The roentgen is a measure of how much charge due to ionization is produced in a volume of air by X and gamma radiation only. The SI unit is the Coloumb/kg. It is not currently in widespread use.

Roentgen equivalent man (rem). Rem is a measure of the amount of biological damage caused by radiation passing through human tissue. Different types and energies of radiation are capable of causing different degrees of damage. For example, alpha radiation is more capable of causing biological damage to the tissues that it interacts with than is gamma radiation. The rem attempts to give an easy way of equating the ability to cause biological damage. Rem is calculated by multiplying Rad by a factor that accounts for the differing abilities to cause damage.

The SI unit is the **sievert (Sv)**. 1 rem = 0.01 Sv or 100 rem = 1 Sv.

The sievert (Sv) and rem are health effects-related measurements of absorbed radiation.

Exposure (Dose) Rate

The exposure (dose) rate is the amount of radiation exposure per unit of time, usually per hour. The exposure rate is generally expressed in roentgens per hour or in milliroentgens per hour on most of the instruments in common use.

Exercise: How Well Do You Know Your Physics?

Purpose: To assess your understanding of basic radiation physics.

Directions: Answer each item. Check your answers in Appendix B. If you missed any items, review this section before continuing on to the next section.

1. How do unstable atoms become stable?

2. Which type of ionizing radiation is the least penetrating?

3. What is the SI unit that measures the amount of radioactive material?

4. What is the unit for radiation absorbed dose in SI units?

5. What are two biological effects units of absorbed radiation?

Radiation Protection Principles

Elements of Radiation Protection

ALARA

This principle states that all efforts be aimed at keeping the radiation exposure **As Low As Reasonably Achievable.** By using these radiation protection principles, emergency department personnel can adequately care for the patient's medical needs while minimizing their own radiation exposure. All activities should be guided by the ALARA concept.

There are three basic radiation protection principles that can be employed to reduce exposure to ionizing radiation. These principles are based on consideration of three radiation protection factors that alter radiation dose: time, distance and shielding.

Time. Time is an important factor in radiation protection. This principle states that the shorter the time spent in a radiation field, the less radiation is absorbed by the body. Depending on the activity present, radioactive material will emit a certain amount of radiation per unit time. Obviously, the longer a person remains in a radiation field, the more radiation the person will absorb into the body.

Distance—Inverse Square Law. The inverse square law states that the radiation dose rate changes inversely by the square of the change in the distance. For example: The dose rate at 3 feet is 20 R/hr. Increase the distance by a factor of 2 (to 6 feet), the dose rate decreases by a factor of 2^2 or 4, and the dose rate is 5 R/hr. Triple the distance from 3 to 9 feet, and the dose decreases by a factor of 3^2 or 9. The dose rate would then go from 20 R/hr to 2.2 R/hr. It also works in reverse—decrease the distance to ½, and the dose rate quadruples. Go from 6 to 3 feet, and the dose rate goes from 5 to 20 R/hr. The farther a person is from the source of radiation, the lower the radiation dose.

Shielding. The denser a material, the greater is its ability to stop the passage of radiation. In most cases, high-density material such as lead is used to shield from radiation. Portable lead or concrete shields are sometimes used when responding to accidents where contamination levels are very high. Some specialty centers for radiation accident management have constructed shielded surgical tables for protection. In emergency management of the contaminated patient, shielding is limited to standard surgical clothing with slight modifications. Surgical clothing will protect the individual against contamination and will also stop the passage of all alpha and some beta radiation. However, it does not stop penetrating gamma radiation. In the hospital emergency department, shielding is limited to anti-contamination measures, and the principles of time and distance are used to reduce radiation exposure. Lead aprons used by X-ray departments are only partially effective as they are too thin.

Emergency Response Exposure Limits

The following are the recommended dose limits for workers performing various emergency services as defined by EPA. These are legally established limits. They should not be considered safe limits that can be accumulated with impunity, because they still contain some risk. Strive to maintain ALARA.

Recommended EPA Limits

The recommended dose for emergency response efforts is a total dose of no more than 25 rems for any single life-threatening emergency. Your facility may mandate even lower levels.

What is the total dose exposure approved by your facility?

Emergency Response Exposure Limits		
Dose Limit (REM)	Activity	Condition
5	All	
10	Protecting valuable property	Lower dose not practical.
25	Lifesaving or protection of large populations	Lower dose not practical.
>25	Lifesaving or protection of large populations	Only on a voluntary basis to persons fully aware of the risks involved.
Source: EMI/FEMA. 1994. *Fundamentals for Radiological Response Team* Course		

Yearly Maximum Permissible Dose for Radiation Workers

The Nuclear Regulatory Commission sets yearly radiation exposure limits for various categories of exposed persons. These are legal limits that are not to be exceeded at any time. These limits are published in the 10 Code of Federal Regulations 20, Occupational Limits for External Exposure.

Yearly Maximum Permissible Dose for Radiation Workers	
Whole Body	5 rem
Hands, forearms, etc.	75 rem
Skin of the whole body	30 rem
Pregnant radiation worker (fetus)	0.5 rem for single exposure
Non-radiation worker on public	0.1 rem
Source: EMI/FEMA. 1994. *Fundamentals for Radiological Response Team* Course	

Exercise: Are You in Danger?

Purpose: To check whether you can apply the basic concepts of radiation protection.

Directions: Answer each question. Check your answers in Appendix B. If you missed any items, review this section before continuing on to the next unit.

True or False

_____1.   The longer a person remains in the radiation field, the more radiation dose the person will accumulate.

_____2.   Surgical clothing will stop the penetrating gamma radiation.

_____3.   Lead is not an effective shield against alpha radiation.

_____4.   The quantity of radiation has little effect on the exposure rate from a given radioactive material.

_____5.   The radiation dose rate increases as your distance from the source decreases.

Types of Radiological Instruments

Human senses do not respond to ionizing radiation, so special instrumentation must be used for radiation detection and measurement. Radiation is detected through instruments such as survey meters or dosimeters. Typical radiation instruments will not detect some of the radionuclides commonly used in medicine, industry, and research, regardless of the amount present inside or spilled from the package. On the other hand, for some radionuclides, even for relatively small amounts in intact packages, the instruments can respond very well. The "None, Some, Good Table" in Appendix C identifies the response capabilities of two commonly used survey instruments for 350 radionuclides. This table applies to the Civil Defense instruments CD V-700 and CD V-715 only. You will learn more about how to read and interpret meters and dosimeters in the classroom course.

Survey Meters (such as CD V-700 and CD V-715)

Survey meters measure **exposure rate** or the intensity of the radiation at the location at some point in time. All radiological survey instruments are rate meters—they read out exposure per unit of time. The survey meter can be compared to a speedometer of a car; both measure relative to time. The survey meter measures radiation exposure rate in roentgens per hour like the speedometer of an automobile records the rate of travel in miles per hour.

The two most commonly used radiation monitoring instruments are the Geiger-Mueller (GM) or Geiger counter, and the ionization chamber. Each of these instruments detects radiation by detecting charged particles (ions) produced by ionizing radiation. The Geiger-Mueller counter is designed to detect low-level radiation, while the ionization chamber is designed for both medium- and high-level measurements. The survey instruments most likely to be available are the CD V-715 ionization survey meter and the CD V-700 G-M survey meter. There are a variety of commercially available instruments, and staff should become familiar with the instruments used in their facility.

Dosimeters, Film Badges, Thermoluminescent dosimeters (TLDs)

The dosimeter measures the total amount of radiation to which you were exposed. These devices are commonly called pocket chambers, pocket dosimeters, and pencil dosimeters. Two commonly distributed Civil Defense meters are the CD V-138 and CD V-742.

Dosimeters are calibrated in roentgens (R) or milliroentgens (mR). The dosimeter can be compared to the odometer in a car. The dosimeter measures the radiation exposure in roentgens or milliroentgens and is like the mileage indicator (odometer) which records the total miles traveled.

The CD V-742 measures gamma exposure to 200 roentgens or 200,000 milliroentgens. It is intended for measuring high levels of exposure. The CD V-138 measures relatively low levels of exposure and has a maximum scale reading of 200 milliroentgens. The CD V-730 has a range of 0 to 20 roentgens, and the CD V-740 (silver clip) has a range of 0 to 100 roentgens. Dosimeters of this type are made to be read directly at the time of the incident without the need to be developed or processed.

A film badge consists of a piece of photographic film in a special holder. It is used to monitor whole-body radiation dose.

The thermoluminescent dosimeter (TLD) is another type of dosimeter that measures the total dose accumulated over the period of exposure.

Film badges and TLDs provide a permanent record of the dose received, but must be processed at a remote site to be read.

Limitations of the Meters

Few of the survey meters can detect or measure alpha or low energy beta radiation without special probes. Many of the meters may not have been properly maintained or calibrated. Personnel must be familiar with the limitations of the types of instruments that they will be using.

Radiation Biology

The biological effects of ionizing radiation are caused by the absorption of radiation energy in the body and distribution of that energy in the body. It is important to understand how radiation affects individual cells within the body. If radiation were to pass straight through living material without leaving any energy behind, it would have no biological effect. The following are basic concepts about cell structure to help understand the effects of radiation on the body.

Basic Concepts of Cell Structure

Cells are the smallest structures capable of maintaining life in humans. They are the living units of the body. Many cells together make up organs, which make up systems, which make up the entire organism. Intercellular supporting and connecting structures connect the cells. Each of the approximately 75 trillion cells in the body performs a specific function. All cells require nutrition and oxygen. This allows for the use of energy to carry out the functions of the cell. All cells also must have the ability to excrete and eliminate waste products. Additionally, cells must have the ability to reproduce, although this may be lost in the maturation process, as in neurons.

The internal environment of the cell consists of the nucleus, the cytoplasm, water, electrolytes, proteins (both structural and enzymes), lipids, and carbohydrates, as shown in the diagram below.

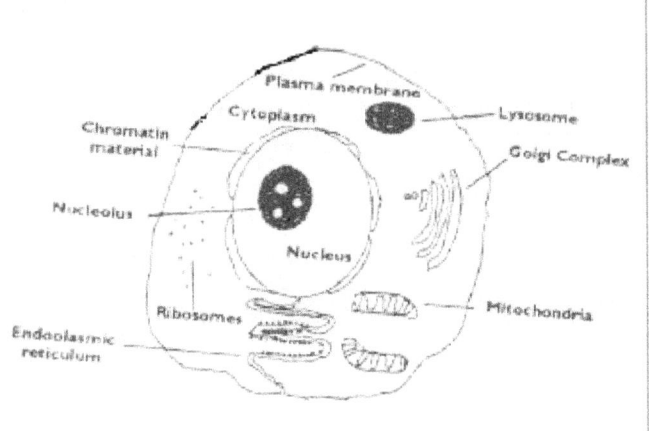

Cell Membrane. Membranes line the cell itself and the structures contained within it. These membranes are not identical but tend to be similar in structure. The cell membrane, or the membrane that contains the entire cell and its contents, consists mostly of lipids with some proteins. The cell membrane is not just an inert bag. It is alive and has many functions, such as controlling what enters and exits the cell, has receptors for hormones, etc. The membrane consists of a bilipid layer with embedded proteins.

Cytoplasm. Cytoplasm is a semi-liquid material that composes cells. It has various specialized structures floating in it and is mostly water.

Nucleus. The nucleus is the largest structure of the cell. It contains chromosomes that carry the cell's genetic information.

DNA and Chromosomes. DNA carried in the chromosomes is the critical site of radiation damage in a cell. It carries, in code form, all of the blueprints that specify a human being: the well-developed brain, the sensitive finger, and the upright stance. It also carries the instructions for the activities and the structure of the cell. The chromosomes are long thread-like structures made up of a complex material called DNA, which is a very long molecule.

DNA is a very large, tightly-coiled, double-stranded molecule that is sensitive to radiation damage. This macromolecule contains the genetic information. The structure of DNA is similar to a ladder. The rungs are made of specific, different molecules (2 required to make a rung), and the sequence of the rung molecules caries the genetic information. Radiation effects can range from complete breaks of one or both of the side chains of the DNA, to point mutations that are essentially radiation-induced chemical changes in the nucleotides that may not affect the integrity of the basic structure, but will change the information coded on the DNA. Mechanisms exist for repair of some types of damage. Other types, such as double strand breaks, have no accurate mechanism for repair.

Types of Cell Damage

When radiation strikes living cells, the radiation energy is transferred to the atoms of the cell, causing chemical changes (ionization) that may be harmful to the cell. The radiation damaged cell can have one of 3 outcomes.

Cell Survives. When there is no damage, or the damage is fully repaired, the cell is not harmed and survives.

Functional Impairment. Damaged cells can be functionally damaged and be unable to carry out their functions, or they may undergo transformation to a cancer cell. This damage may not appear immediately, but may occur over a long period of time.

Cell Death. Most organs have a fairly large reserve capacity. Killed cells are replaced quickly in most tissues with any degree of reserve capacity, and do not cause significant overall clinical effects unless the cells involved are highly critical or the fraction of cells killed in a given organ is large. In some cases, the immature precursor cells that produce the functional, mature cells are more radiosensitive than the mature cell. One instance is the bone marrow, where the stem cells are much more radiosensitive than the mature red blood cells or the granulocytes. For this reason, it can take days to weeks for the damage to become clinically apparent. If sufficient numbers of cells die, the structural or functional integrity of an organ is affected.

Tissue Sensitivities

The amount of radiation-induced damage to tissues is influenced by the tissue sensitivity.

Most Sensitive

The most sensitive tissues are:

- Lymphocytes
- Bone marrow stem cells
- Small intestine epithelium

Some tissues, such as the epithelial lining of the gastrointestinal tract, and the hematopoietic system in the bone marrow, maintain a continuous high cell turnover rate. Thus, the stem cells are almost all relatively sensitive to radiation. These tissues normally contain cell populations in all stages of maturation and differentiation from primitive stem cells to mature functional cells. Bone marrow has a large reserve capacity in adults. In general, sensitivity to ionizing radiation is higher in immature, primitive and rapidly reproducing cells such as bone marrow stem cells and intestinal epithelial cells. Mature cells, and cells that do not reproduce are more resistant to the effects of radiation. One exception is mature lymphocytes, which are mature cells that do not reproduce, but are exceptionally sensitive to the effects of radiation.

Least Sensitive

The least sensitive tissues are:
- Central nervous system
- Bone cells
- Muscle cells

These cells are mature functional cells that are relatively resistant. The functional cells of the central nervous system (neurons) are not replaced if lost or destroyed.

Mechanisms of Biological Damage

Biological damage can occur through direct and indirect action.

Direct Action

The direct action mechanism occurs because of direct insult to a biological molecule by ionizing radiation and the consequent break-up of the molecule. The chromosomes are the critical site of radiation damage in a cell.

Indirect Action

The indirect mechanism occurs when water in the body is irradiated. The water molecule is split and the resulting free radicals or peroxides will then damage the cell.

Factors Affecting Biological Damage

Total Dose, as you learned earlier, is the quantity of radiation absorbed. The greater the dose, the greater the damage.

Dose Rate. Biological systems have mechanisms for repair of damage caused by radiation. All of these mechanisms have a saturation point, however. If the dose rate is low enough that the repair mechanisms can keep up, most of the damage will be repaired and clinical effects will be minimized. Theoretically, the damage should be zero in this case, but no biological system is perfect, and repairs will occasionally be faulty, or damage will escape repair. Any damage to the genetic material that is present at replication will be passed on. If the dose rate is such that the damage rate outstrips the repair rate, then damage will accumulate.

Type and Energy of Radiation. Alpha radiation does not penetrate the skin, so it is not a hazard if the source is outside the body. If internalized, however, it transfers its energy in a short distance, doing a great deal of damage. If the alpha particle is released next to a cell's nucleus, a great deal of damage can be done to the genetic material. Beta radiation is a hazard to the skin if external, but will not damage the internal organs unless the source is taken internally. It does not transfer its energy in as short a distance as alpha, but will do a significant degree of damage. Gamma radiation will penetrate deeply from externally or internally, reaching deep organs. Generally, the greater the energy of the radiation, the greater the damage it will do.

Portion of Body Exposed. Different tissues have different sensitivities to radiation (bone marrow, gut, epithelium are most sensitive; bone, brain, etc. are least sensitive). If the portion of the body exposed contains sensitive tissue, then the degree of damage will be higher than if it contains a less sensitive tissue. An isolated limb can tolerate a much greater exposure than the trunk. The greater the percent of the body exposed, the less tolerated the damage. This would be analogous to a crushed small toe being much better tolerated than a crushed leg.

Biological Variability (age, general health, etc.). The extremes of age are the most sensitive to damage due to radiation. The young are sensitive due to their high rate of growth and cell division; the elderly are sensitive to radiation damage due to their generally poorer reserves and their decreased ability to handle biological stress. People who are in better general health will have a greater ability to tolerate radiation or any other biological stress.

Availability of Treatment. As with any disease or injury, greater quantity and sophistication of treatment leads to a better outcome. This becomes more important in incidents involving a large number of patients (mass casualty incidents), and incidents that occur in less developed countries.

Clinical Effects of Radiation

Acute Radiation Syndrome (ARS)

Acute radiation syndrome (ARS) is a disease state that occurs in stages over hours to months as damage to organs and tissues is expressed. It can be further divided into the hematopoietic, the gastrointestinal, and the cardiovascular/central nervous system syndromes based on the clinical picture. This group of signs and symptoms develops as a result of an acute, or in some cases subacute, exposure of the whole or a significant portion of the body to an appreciable dose (> 100 REM) of ionizing radiation. The syndrome is a clinical manifestation of the responses of the individual constituents of the body systems to an acute exposure to radiation. The clinical course is predictable and is divided into prodrome, latent, manifest illness, and recovery or death phases that are of variable duration (a few hours to several weeks), depending on the nature of the exposure. A general rule of thumb is that the higher the dose, the more rapid the onset of symptoms, the shorter each phase will be, and the more intense the symptoms. For example, the patient who develops mild nausea several hours after the exposure has probably received a fairly low dose, while the patient who develops severe vomiting and diarrhea within several minutes of the exposure has received a very high, probably fatal dose. These observations can be used to make very rough initial dose estimations. The LD $_{50-60}$ is about 450 RAD. LD $_{50-60}$ is the dose at which 50 percent of the people exposed will be expected to die within 60 days of exposure without treatment.

ARS—Prodrome Phase is the first phase of ARS. It consists of non-specific symptoms such as malaise, anorexia, nausea, vomiting and possibly diarrhea. Onset will be in minutes to hours to a day or more, and lasts hours to days. This is the phase during which emergency department and field personnel will see these patients. The more intense and the more rapid the onset, the greater the dose.

ARS—Latent Stage is the second stage of ARS. The symptoms of the prodrome phase resolve except for some mild weakness. This stage will last for hours to days to a few weeks. In general, the shorter the latent stage, the greater the dose.

ARS—Manifest Illness Stage is the third stage. This is the stage where the damage to the organs and tissues becomes manifest. It is further divided into 3 syndromes based on the clinical picture as outlined below.

Hematopoietic Syndrome. Occurs in doses in the 1-8 Gy range.

The prodrome consists of anorexia, nausea, vomiting and possibly diarrhea, and may take up to 2–4 hours to 1-2 days to begin. The latent phase lasts 3-4 weeks and progresses to the manifest illness stage. The patient will become severely ill as the damage to the bone marrow becomes clinically apparent. The clinical picture is one of bone marrow suppression with leukopenia (low white blood cell count), thrombocytopenia (low platelet counts) and anemia. Serious, difficult to treat infections, anemia, difficult to control bleeding, poor wound healing, etc. will result. These patients require intensive treatment and possibly bone marrow stimulating factors or bone marrow transplants.

Gastrointestinal Syndrome. Occurs in doses in the 8-30 Gy range.

The prodrome consists of severe nausea, vomiting with watery diarrhea onset within 1–3 hours or less. The latent phase may last 5-7 days, and is followed by the manifest illness phase. The patient will develop a return of severe nausea, vomiting and diarrhea, likely bloody with fever. The clinical picture is one of significant damage to the gastrointestinal tract, mainly the small intestine lining. The epithelial lining of the gut is depleted, leading to invasion of gut bacteria into the wall of the intestine, and then into the blood as well as bleeding from these denuded areas. Absorptive capacity is also lost, leading to malnutrition, dehydration and electrolyte disturbances. The doses that produce the gastrointestinal syndrome are higher than those required to produce the hematopoietic syndrome; therefore, these patients will also sustain extensive the bone marrow damage characteristic of the hematopoietic syndrome. Their condition will be further complicated by the resultant infections from gut bacteria, as well as the bleeding from the gut being made more difficult to control by the falling white blood cell and platelet counts, and the anemia. These patients will require very intensive treatments if they are going to survive, and many will eventually die of their illnesses.

Cardiovascular/Central Nervous System (CV/CNS) Syndrome. Occurs at doses over 30 Gy.

The prodrome consists of a rapid onset of severe nausea, vomiting and diarrhea followed rapidly by confusion, seizures, coma, and hypotension progressing to death within 24–48 hours. If present, the latent phase will also be very short. These doses are high enough to produce damage to the radioresistant central nervous system and cardiovascular system. Doses of this magnitude are essentially universally fatal.

ARS—Recovery or Death is the fourth and final stage during which the patient either recovers, or dies from injuries sustained.

Treatment of the Acute Radiation Syndrome

As emergency department and field personnel will be treating patients during the prodrome phase if they see the manifestations of ARS at all, treatment will be mainly symptomatic. Measures such as IV fluids to replace fluid losses from vomiting and diarrhea, antiemetics to control nausea and vomiting and other comfort measures are indicated. Further treatment of ARS, as well as treatment of contamination and incorporation, are beyond the scope of this course, and will be covered in the classroom course.

Treatment Priorities

In the treatment of the patient involved in a radiological accident, the treatment of conventional (non-radiological) traumatic and medical problems takes precedence over treatment of the radiological injuries. ARS is rarely a life-threat in the E.D. If it is, the patient has most likely received a fatal dose for which there is no effective treatment beyond comfort measures. Conventional life-threats, such as a tension pneumothorax, however, are treatable and survivable, making these first priority.

Dose Estimation

There are several methods to determine the dose of ionizing radiation that a patient has received. The most accurate would be to read the dose off of a dosimeter if the patient were wearing one at the time of the exposure. If not, there are other methods to estimate dose.

1. **Clinical Effects** As stated above, the intensity and rapidity of onset of symptoms is related to the dose, and this can be used to estimate the dose received.

2. **Cytogenetic Dosimetry** Some type of damage to the chromosomes is characteristic of ionizing radiation. Blood can be drawn from the patient, and the number of these damaged chromosomes can be used to estimate the dose received.

3. **Absolute Lymphocyte Count (ALC)** The ALC at 48 hours can be used to estimate the severity and lethality of the dose received.

Chemical Hazards

There are other hazards associated with radiation. For instance, a radioactive substance may also be corrosive, flammable, or toxic. In fact, it is possible that these hazards may pose a greater threat than the ionizing radiation. The hazards may occur because of direct exposure or through the interactions of the materials with each other or with a radioactive material.

Exposure to chemicals can be acute or chronic. Acute means a single dose or exposure, whereas chronic means repeated exposure. Exposure may be local or systemic. Local means that the chemical attacks at the site of exposure. Systemic means that the chemical must pass through the skin, mucous membranes, or lungs and will move through the bloodstream.

Chemicals do not present any fixed symptoms that are unique to all chemical exposures; instead, symptoms of exposure to each type of chemical vary considerably. The following table lists some of the effects of chemical hazards on the body.

Effects of Chemicals on the Body	
Systems	**Symptoms**
• Lungs	• Eye irritation
• Nervous system	• Respiratory (lungs) distress
• Hepatic (liver)	• Asphyxiation
• Hematic (blood)	• Unconsciousness
• Kidneys	• Fatigue, exhaustion, irritability
• Skeletal (bones)	• Headaches
• Dermal (skin)	• Nausea

Nature of Chemical Hazards

The hazards posed by chemicals vary and pose many kinds of threats and problems. Chemicals can occur as aerosol, dust, fumes, gas, smoke, and vapors. For example, hazards can occur when radioactive materials combine with flammables or explosives. In such situations, chemicals will intensify a fire and will cause the release of more radioactive material. Many radioactive materials are shipped as corrosives. The toxic gas uranium hexafluoride is more hazardous than the uranium radiation. Shipments of uranium hexafluoride can have both "radioactive" and "corrosive" labels. Metals such as uranium and plutonium are heavy metals and will have toxic effects similar to other heavy metals such as lead and mercury.

 **References**

FEMA, NFA, United States Fire Administration. 1995. *Basic Life Support and Hazardous Materials Response,* Emmitsburg, MD.

FEMA, EMI. 1997. *Fundamentals Course for Radiological Response Teams. Student Manual.* Emmitsburg, MD.

FEMA, EPA, DOT. 1993. *Hazardous Materials Workshop for Hospital Staff.* Emmitsburg, MD.

FEMA, EMI. 1984. *Hospital Emergency Department Management of Radiation Accidents.* Emmitsburg, MD (out of print).

International Atomic Energy Commission. 1988. *The Radiological Accident in Goiania.* Vienna.

Kuehl, A. (Ed.). 1994. *Prehospital Systems and Medical Oversight. National Association of Emergency Physicians.* Mosby-Year Book, Inc. St. Louis, MO.

NUREG-1458 1992. *Emergency Response to a Highway Accident in Springfield, Massachusetts on December 16, 1991.* Washington, D.C.

Sherman, J. 1988. *Chemical Exposure and Disease.* Van Nostrand Reinhold. New York, NY.

U.S. Environmental Protection Agency. 1993. *Radiation: Risks and Realities.* Washington, D.C.

U.S. Nuclear Regulatory Commission. 1995. *Annual Report, 1994-FY1995, Nuclear Materials.* Office of Operational Data. Washington, D.C.

UNIT 5: POST-TEST

Directions: Answer each question. Each answer counts 10 points. Check your answers in Appendix B. If you missed any items, review this unit before taking the final examination.

1. John used a survey meter to measure the amount of radiation present and found none. Later, Sue used a different same meter and found significant amounts of radiation. What could have caused the differences in the readings?

   a) John's meter was not working properly.

   b) Radiation had time to register in the body because of the time that passed between the two readings.

   c) Sue's body or clothing were contaminated with radioactive material.

   d) John did not use the proper type of meter to detect the type of radiation being emitted.

2. Which of the following would expose deep organs to radiation?

   a) Chest X-rays
   b) Gamma rays
   c) Beta particles
   d) Alpha particles

3. Which of the following is the highest source of radiation (on an annual basis)?
   a) Living in Chicago

   b) X-rays and nuclear medicine

   c) Living near a nuclear power plant

   d) Radon in an average household

4. What is the largest source of man-made radiation?
   a) Radiation used in medicine

   b) Nuclear power plants

   c) Scientific research

   d) Mining

5. Which of the following takes priority in the treatment?

   a) Nausea and vomiting caused by exposure to 15 Gy external irradiation.

   b) Tension pneumothorax.

   c) Superficial leg laceration.

   d) Decontamination

6. Which of the following particles pose an external and internal hazard?

   a) Beta particles

   b) Alpha particles

   c) Beta particles and gamma rays

   d) Electrons

7. The rad, rem, and gray are measures of what?

   a) Absorbed Dose

   b) Units of Exposure

   c) Amount of Radioactivity

   d) Degrees of radiation

8. An important goal of emergency responders in dealing with radiation-related incidents is to:

   a) Protect the public

   b) Save lives

   c) Keep their own radiation exposure ALARA

   d) Treat all patients as emergency care victims

9. What is the EPA recommended maximum dose limit for any single life-threatening emergency?

   a) 5

   b) 10

   c) 25

   d) 50

10. What happens at the fourth stage in the acute radiation syndrome?

    a) Recovery or death
    b) Nausea and diarrhea
    c) Weakness
    d) Gastrointestinal syndrome

UNIT 6:

Final Evaluation

Overview

This unit contains the final examination for this course. Please circle the correct answer.

Answers to this exam can be found in Appendix B.

Unit 6: Final Evaluation

FINAL EVALUATION

Directions: Read each item carefully and select the correct answer.

1. Which of the following statements best describes a hospital's involvement in hazardous materials and events?

    a) Hospitals are seldom involved in hazardous materials incidents.
    b) A hospital's primary purpose is to help diagnose the nature of the hazardous chemical.
    c) A hospital's involvement primarily centers around the decontamination of patients.
    d) A hospital's involvement in hazardous materials incidents may take many forms, including diagnosis of the hazardous material and treatment of contaminated patients.

2. Compliance issues regarding hazardous materials are designated by which of the following groups?

    a) State and local transportation agencies
    b) The Joint Commission for the Accreditation of Hospitals
    c) EPA, NRC, and OSHA
    d) FBI, DOT, FEMA

3. A chemical that causes a sudden, almost instantaneous release of pressure, gas, and heat when subjected to sudden shock, pressure, or high temperatures best describes which type of DOT hazardous materials classification?

    a) Class 2—Gases
    b) Class 1—Explosives
    c) Class 6—Toxic (poisonous) materials and infectious substances
    d) Class 7—Radioactive materials

4. What type of injury is not likely to occur from a chemical?

    a) Bone damage
    b) Severe and deep tissue burns
    c) Eye damage
    d) Laceration or puncture to the skin

Unit 6: Final Evaluation

5. Which of the following is most likely to be a source of hazardous materials within the home?

   a) Recycled garbage
   b) Household cleaning products
   c) Heating pad
   d) Lawnmower

6. What is the purpose of a hospital emergency/disaster response plan?

   a) It describes the policies and procedures that should be followed in the event of a hazardous materials incident.
   b) It's a reference tool for external responders to an emergency.
   c) It ensures that the hospital is in compliance with OSHA regulations.
   d) It's a training tool for hospital personnel.

7. Which of the following statements best describes what procedure should be followed by the person first responding to a hazardous materials event call?

   a) Refer the call to the safety officer.
   b) Contact the security officer immediately.
   c) Assume the victim(s) are contaminated until proven otherwise—and base any actions on that assumption.
   d) Notify the hospital's admission office of potential patients' arrival.

8. Under what circumstances is respiratory isolation necessary when dealing with hazardous materials events?

   a) When radioactive contamination is suspected
   b) When hazardous materials emit vapors or gases
   c) When hazardous materials contamination is known or suspected.
   d) During the hospital evacuation

9. What is the purpose of a control zone?

   a) To establish an area for the reception of contaminated patients
   b) To differentiate the controlled (contaminated) area from the noncontrolled (uncontaminated) area
   c) To control the flow of traffic into the hospital
   d) To set up barriers to prevent the media's access

Unit 6: Final Evaluation

10. When should you use Level C personal protection equipment?

    a) When the highest level of respiratory, skin, eye, and mucous membrane protection is needed
    b) When only minimal skin protection is required
    c) When you don't need much skin and eye protection
    d) When you don't require a high level of respiratory protection

11. Under what conditions would you take samples of emesis, sputum, and urine?

    a) When external contamination is suspected
    b) When internal contamination is suspected
    c) When you need to locate contaminated areas
    d) When there is the possibility of a lawsuit for incorrect actions

12. What is gross decontamination?

    a) Cross-contamination
    b) A type of secondary decontamination
    c) A lethal contaminant
    d) The removal or chemical alteration of the majority of a contaminant

13. If you remove the biological (etiologic) contamination hazards through destroying microorganisms and their toxins, what mechanism of decontamination did you use?

    a) Emulsification
    b) Disposal
    c) Disinfection
    d) Absorption

14. What is the name of a reference tool that is produced by chemical manufacturers that provides information on the chemical identity of the hazardous material, its known acute and chronic effects, and exposure limits, among other things?

    a) The Emergency Response Guidebook for Selected Hazardous Materials
    b) Chemical Hazards Information Response System
    c) Material Safety Data Sheet
    d) CHEMTREC

Unit 6: Final Evaluation

15.   Which of the following is an inaccurate statement regarding radiation?

    a) X-rays are a significant source of radiation.
    b) More than 80 percent of our exposure to radiation comes from natural sources.
    c) Radiation comes from outer space, the ground, and even from our own bodies.
    d) There was no radiation present prior to 1944.

16.   If you have an diagnostic X-ray, then you have been:

    a) Externally irradiated
    b) Contaminated
    c) Made radioactive.
       d) Exposed to potentially lethal doses of radiation

17.   Alpha and beta particles and gamma rays are examples of:

    a) Atoms
    b) Ionizing radiation
    c) Neutrons
    d) Isotopes

18.   The SI unit for quantity of radioactive material is:

    a) Becquerel
    b) Millicurie
    c) Microcurie
    d) Curie

19.   How is the exposure rate generally expressed?

    a) In Roentgens per hour
    b) In Gray
    c) In Radiation absorbed dose
    d) In Microcurie

20.   How can you reduce the exposure to ionizing radiation?

    a) Stand at least two inches away from the radiation source.
    b) Spend as little time as possible in a radiation field.
    c) Avoid standing next to a metal doorway.
    d) Don't live near a nuclear facility.

APPENDIX A

CHEMICAL/RADIATION EVENT EMERGENCY PLAN ADDENDUM

COUNTY GENERAL HOSPITAL

1997

CHEMICAL/RADIATION EVENT EMERGENCY PLAN ADDENDUM

TABLE OF CONTENTS

COUNTY GENERAL HOSPITAL
CHEMICAL/RADIATION EVENT EMERGENCY PLAN ADDENDUM

I. OBJECTIVES - CHEMICAL/RADIATION EVENT PLAN

The purpose in developing this procedure is to ensure that the staff of County General Hospital will maintain a high degree of preparedness in the event of a Chemical/Radiation Event Emergency.

Through this plan there is offered protection to life by making maximum use of available manpower, equipment, and other resources during a Chemical/Radiation Event Emergency.

The hospital administration and staff is committed to cooperating with local, state and federal agencies in responding to Chemical/Radiation emergencies, as well as supporting inservice training and drills. Serious medical problems will always have priority over concerns about <u>radiation</u> such as radiation monitoring, contamination control and decontamination. Instructions for <u>chemical</u> contamination events will be followed according to authorities.

II. NOTIFICATION AND VERIFICATION RESPONSIBILITIES

A. FRONT DESK

1. Contact Nursing Supervisor or Emergency Department nurse to receive call.

B. NURSING SUPERVISOR OR EMERGENCY DEPARTMENT NURSE RESPONSIBILITIES

1. Receive information regarding chemical/radiological accident
    a. Number of accident victims
    b. Each victim's medical status
    c. If the victims have been surveyed for contamination
    d. Status of victims EXPOSED versus CONTAMINATED
    e. Identification of contaminant if known
    f. Estimated time of arrival
    g. Advise ambulance personnel of entrance to be used
    h. If accident notification comes from a source other than 9-1-1 or ambulance crew, obtain a call-back number and verify the accident before assembling the Chemical/Radiological Emergency Response Team and preparing for patient admission.

2. Delegate the Front Desk to initiate call for the appropriate personnel (i.e., Chemical/Radiological Emergency Response Team, Trauma Team, Medical Alert Plan, etc.). Contact Administration as appropriate.

3. Delegate the Front Desk to overhead page "Medical Alert, Code Yellow" x 3. Chemical/Radiation Contamination Incident will be designated as "Code Yellow."

4. Notify or delegate Administration to notify appropriate offices:

    County EMS: 842-3412 or 9-1-1

    Chem-Trec: 1-800-424-9300 (Emergency Response Guidebook - ED) (Yellow DOT Book)

    State: 1-800-452-0311, or

Radiation Control Section, State Health Division: 1-229-5797

Poison Control: 1-800-452-7165

Federal (DOE - Department of Energy): Call 1-800-452-0311

REAC/TS (Radiation Emergency Assistance Center/Training Site): 423-481-1000, ext. 1502 (8:00-4:30 EST or Beeper #241 on weekends and holidays)

C. Organizational Chart (see page 4)

III. CHEMICAL/RADIATION HAZARDS EMERGENCY RESPONSE TEAM

A. TRAUMA TEAM

1. NURSING SUPERVISOR
    a. Lead, advise, and coordinate the facility
    b. Notify appropriate State and/or Federal agencies
    c. Assume duties of Administration until their arrival
    d. Communicate with Administration for coordination
    e. Ensure communication with family members

2. EMERGENCY DEPARTMENT NURSE (Triage) (team coordinator)
    a. Lead, advise and coordinate E.D.
        (1) Assist with preparation of the Chemical/Radiation Emergency Area(C/REA)
        (2) Assume primary responsibility in caring for the chemical/radiation accident victim(s)
    b. LIMIT PERSONNEL in area; define roles before patient arrival. No pregnant personnel in area.
    c. Assume duties of Nursing Supervisor until his/her arrival

3. EMERGENCY DEPARTMENT PHYSICIAN (Triage) (team coordinator)
    a. Diagnose, treat, provide emergency medical care

4. LABORATORY
    a. Obtain or receive lab specimens that need to be run immediately

5. RADIOLOGY
    a. Operate portable unit as needed
    **b. Monitor and document for radiation events
    c. Obtain survey equipment if Radiation Safety Officer (RSO) or Nuclear Medicine technician not available.

6. RESPIRATORY THERAPY/E.K.G.
    a. Provide routine patient care as needed

7. ADDITIONAL EMERGENCY DEPARTMENT NURSES
    a. Assist with preparation of C/REA
    b. Assist with medical procedures
    c. Collect specimens
    d. Assist with decontamination
    e. Assess patient's needs and intervene appropriately

B. ADDITIONAL PHYSICIANS AS NEEDED

1. Diagnose, treat, and provide emergency medical care

C. EMTs (AS AVAILABLE)

   1. Assist with medical procedures

   2. Assist with documentation

D. TECHNICAL RECORDER (Medical records and/or Patient Business Office person)

   1. Record admitting and medical data

**E. RADIATION SAFETY OFFICER (Radiologist and/or Nuclear Medicine technician)

   1. Monitor patient and area

   2. Advise on contamination and exposure control

   3. Maintain survey equipment

F. ADMINISTRATION (President, Vice President, and/or Vice President of Patient Services

   1. Notify appropriate Local, State and/or Federal agencies. (See pages A-1,2.)

   2. Coordinate hospital responses

   3. Assure ongoing hospital operations

   4. Public information officer
      a. Releases information to public media

   5. Coordinate all equipment, blood products, and supplies as needed.

G. PLANT SERVICES MANAGER (or designee)

   1. Maintenance
      a. Set up contamination control areas
         (1) Bring "Chemical/Radiation Decontamination cart" to Emergency Department Lobby
            (kept in basement oxygen storage room)
         (2) Prepare Chemical/Radiation Emergency Area (C/REA)
      b. Deliver appropriate supplies

   2. Housekeeping/Laundry
      a. Deliver appropriate linens and supplies
      b. Assist with area contamination control setup

   3. Security personnel
      a. Secure chemical/radiation emergency area
      b. Secure hospital entrances
      c. Control crowds

H. PURCHASING

    1. Bring "Chemical/Radiation Decontamination Box" with supplies to Emergency (box kept in Purchasing).

    2. Be available for additional needed supplies

I. FRONT DESK

    1. Route all accident related calls to administrative person or designee

    2. Supply additional personnel to handle paper work and/or phones

COUNTY GENERAL HOSPITAL ORGANIZATION CHART

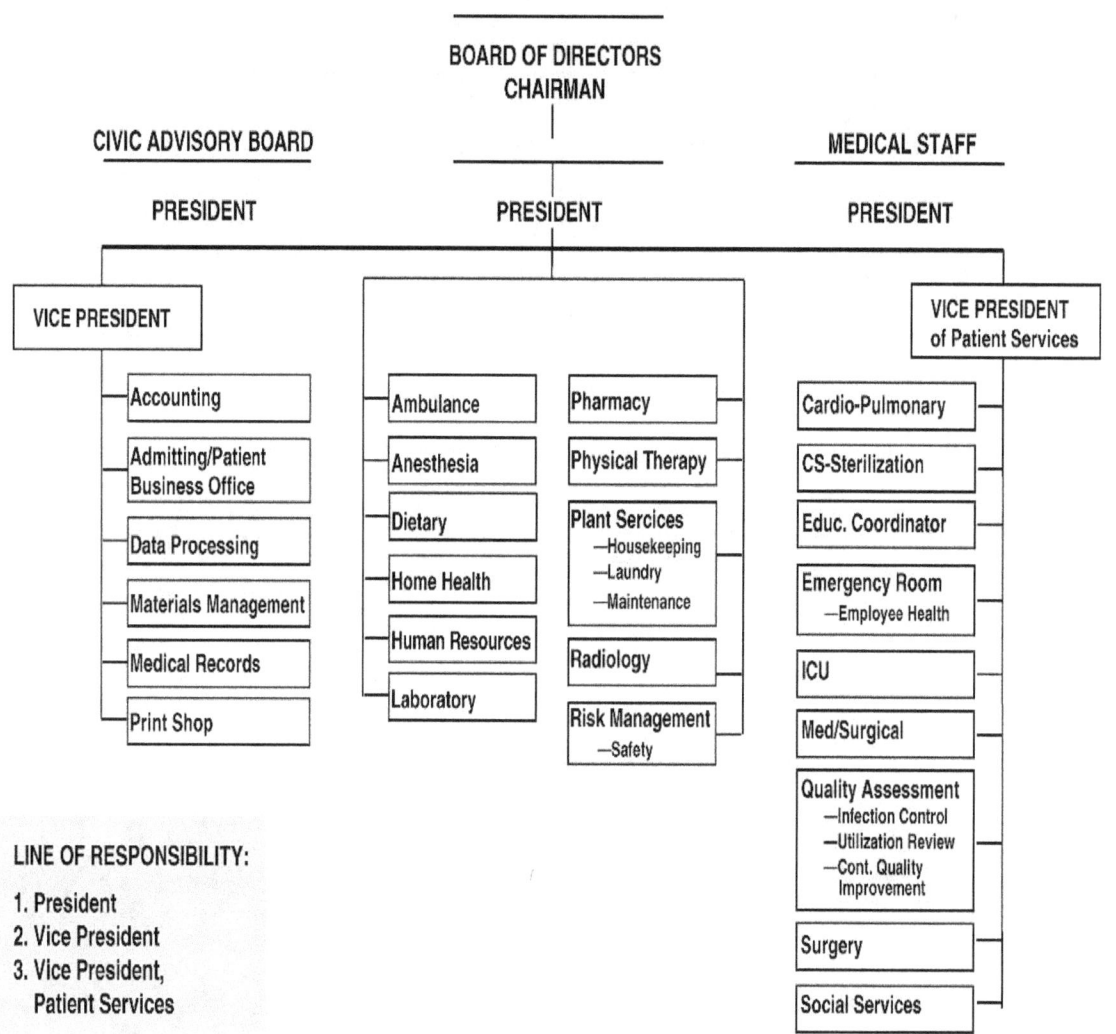

COUNTY GENERAL HOSPITAL
ORGANIZATIONAL CHART

BOARD OF DIRECTORS
CHAIRMAN

CIVIC ADVISORY BOARD   MEDICAL STAFF

PRESIDENT   PRESIDENT   PRESIDENT

VICE PRESIDENT   VICE PRESIDENT
of Patient Services

Accounting   Ambulance   Pharmacy   Cardio-Pulmonary

Admitting/Patient
Business Office   Anesthesia   Physical Therapy   CS-Sterilization

Data Processing   Dietary   Plant Sercices
—Housekeeping
—Laundry
—Maintenance   Educ. Coordinator

Materials Management   Home Health   Emergency Room
—Employee Health

Medical Records   Human Resources   Radiology   ICU

Print Shop   Laboratory   Risk Management
—Safety   Med/Surgical

Quality Assessment
—Infection Control
—Utilization Review
—Cont. Quality
Improvement

Surgery

Social Services

LINE OF RESPONSIBILITY:

1. President
2. Vice President
3. Vice President,
   Patient Services

IV. PREPARATION OF CHEMICAL/RADIATION EMERGENCY AREA (C/REA)

    A. DECONTAMINATION AREA

        1. Attach hose to faucet in Laundry; run hose out to back parking lot. (Plant Services)

        2. Place large empty water container (wading pool) with drain hose in decontamination area (Plant Services)

        3. Direct hose into drain (Plant Services)

        4. Screen off decontamination area for privacy if possible (Plant Services)

    B. HOSPITAL ENTRANCE TO TRAUMA ROOM

        1. Cover floor and/or ground from ambulance or transport vehicle to trauma room, or appropriate area, with 3-4 foot wide brown paper, butcher paper, or other appropriate material – ½ width of walkway (Plant Services)

        2. Securely tape paper with 2 inch masking tape (Plant Services)

        3. Cover door handles and light switches (Plant Services)

        4. Access to area LIMITED and controlled by security officers (Plant Services)

    C. TRAUMA ROOM (Bed #4, unless otherwise designated)

        1. Remove all unnecessary equipment, supplies (Plant Services/E.D. personnel)
            a. Remove regular bed or table if different stretcher to be used

        2. Remove patients and/or non-essential personnel (E.D. personnel)

        3. Cover remaining equipment and/or supplies with sheets or plastic (Plant Services and Emergency Department Staff)
            a. Cover door handles and light switches (Plant Services)

        4. Cover floor of C/REA (all treatment areas) with 3-4 foot wide brown paper, butcher paper, or other appropriate material (Plant Services)

        5. Securely tape paper with 2 inch masking tape (Plant Services)

        6. Rope off area and mark "Chemical/Radiation Area" (Plant Services)

        7. Mark floor with tape to designate contaminated versus clean area (Plant Services)

        8. No eating or drinking in C/REA (All Personnel)

        9. Access to C/REA limited and all entrances/exits controlled by security personnel or locked doors (Plant Services)

      10. Post "No pregnant" signs at all appropriate entrances.

D. EQUIPMENT AND SUPPLIES (found in E.D., Purchasing, Plant Services, Housekeeping, and Radiology)

1. Chemical/Radiation Decontamination Cart (Plant Services)
    a. Bleach (sodium hypochlorite) (1 quart)
    b. Boraxo - powdered (2 boxes)
    c. Lava Soap (2 bars)
    d. Lead pigs (8 small)
    e. Sheets for equipment drapes (10)
    f. 2" masking tape (2 rolls)
    g. Barrier standards with rope (4)
    h. Large trash bags (10)
    i. Small trash bags (10)
    j. Small ziplock bags (10)
    k. Large ziplock bags (10)
    l. Clipboards with anatomical charts (5)
    m. Wax or felt pens (6)
    n. Skin markers (5)
    o. Signs "RADIATION AREA" (6)
    p. Signs "No Pregnant" (6)
    q. Large bio-medical boxes with liners (6)
    r. Radioactive labels
    s. "D" Batteries (4)

2. Chemical/Radiation Contamination Box (Purchasing)
    a. .9 Na Cl - 1000ml (1 case)
    b. Sterile H_2O - 1000ml (1 case)
    c. 2" tape (6)
    d. Isolation Gowns (1 case)
    e. Head covers (1 case)
    f. Gloves (1 case)
    g. Shoe covers (1 case)
    h. Mild soap
    i. Shield, mask/eye (1 case)
    j. Large disposable drapes (5)
    k. Bi-citra 30cc/water - 30cc

3. Supplies in E.D.
    a. Culture swabs in plastic bags (20)
    b. Trash cans with plastic liners
    c. Surgical scrub soap
    d. Soft scrub brush
    e. 3% hydrogen peroxide

4. House cleaning supplies
    a. Linen (sheets, blankets, towels, patient gowns)

5. May place instruments inside plastic bag to ensure they do not become contaminated.

E. EMERGENGY MEDICAL SUPPLIES

1. Code Cart

2. Suction, oxygen, I.V. solutions, etc.

**F. RADIATION SURVEY EQUIPMENT (Radiation Safety Officer)

1. Ludlum G-M survey meter or other equivalent multi-range survey meter (Nuclear Medicine)
   a. Cover probe with rubber glove

2. Ionization chamber/Dose Calibrator (remains in Nuclear Medicine)

3. Dosimeters (when available)

4. Alpha detector (optional)

G. HOSPITAL FLOOR PLAN (see page A-9)

V. PREPARATION OF CHEMICAL/RADIOLOGICAL EMERGENCY RESPONSE TEAM

A. PROTECTIVE CLOTHING

1. Don protective clothing before patients arrive

2. Wear scrub suit, isolation gown, surgical hoods or head covers, masks, gloves, eye covers, and waterproof shoe covers

3. All open seams and cuffs should be taped with masking tape (2")

4. Two (2) pairs of surgical gloves must be worn
   a. First pair taped to gown
   b. Second pair easily removable (replace if they become contaminated)
   c. Three (3) pairs may be worn for added protection if you wish

**5. Film badges if available

**6. Radiation dosimeter assigned to each team member (when available)
   a. Attach to outside of gown at the neck for easy removal and readings
   b. Dosimeters should be read every 15 to 20 minutes by the RSO or designee
      (1) Document individual readings
      (2) Persons reading above 100 mR/hr. should leave the area as soon as possible following proper exiting procedure

B. ANATOMICAL READING FORM (see page A-10)

C. DOSIMETER READING FORM (see page A-11)

COUNTY GENERAL HOSPITAL FLOOR PLAN GRAPHIC

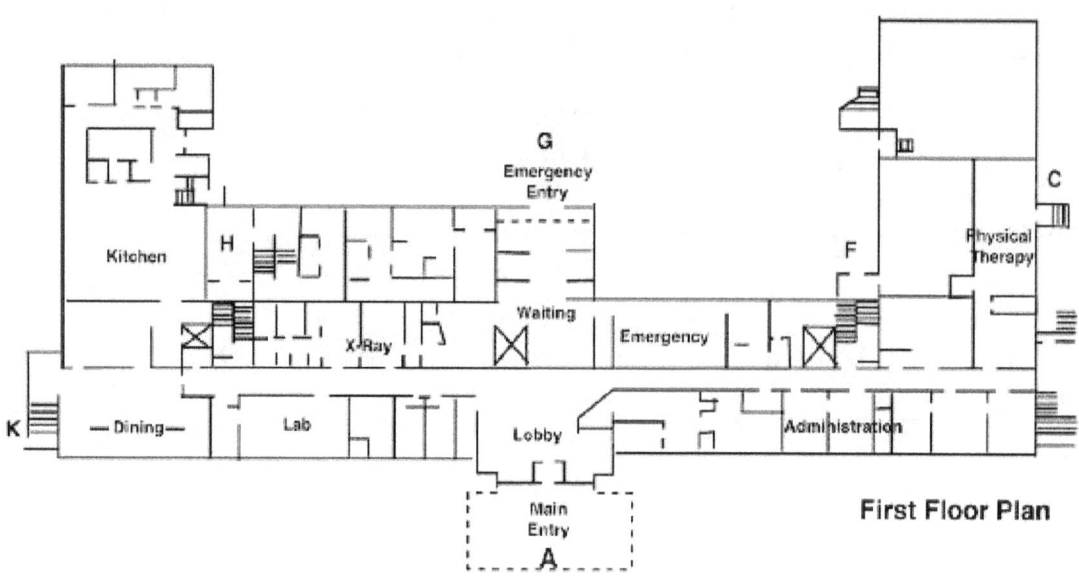

First Floor Plan

1" = 40' 0"

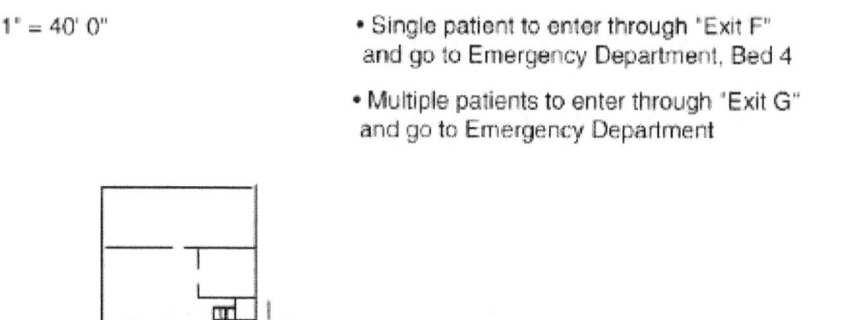

- Single patient to enter through "Exit F" and go to Emergency Department, Bed 4

- Multiple patients to enter through "Exit G" and go to Emergency Department

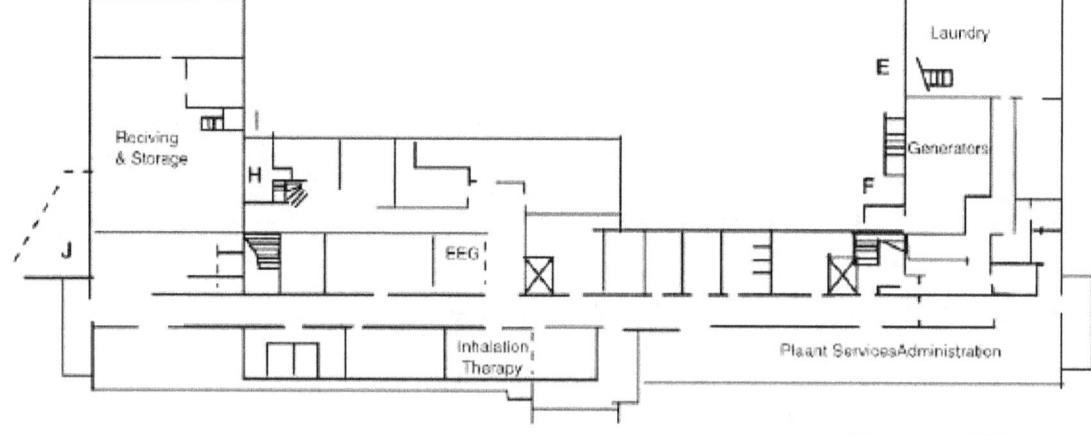

Basement Plan

COUNTY GENERAL HOSPITAL FLOOR PLAN

ANATOMICAL RECORD FORM

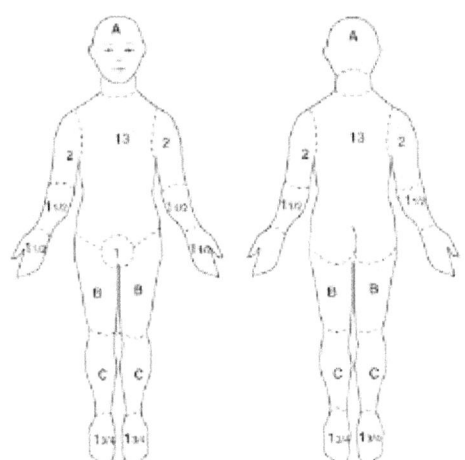

Anatomical Record Form

Date	Time	Reading	Body Location	Treatment, etc.

DOSIMETER LOG TABLE

DOSIMETER LOG

Should be read
every 15 minutes

Date	Time	Name	Dosimeter #	Dosimeter Reading	Date/Time Dosimeter Use Dc'd	Final Reading

VI.   CARE OF THE CHEMICAL/RADIATION ACCIDENT PATIENT ON ARRIVAL

   A.   PATIENT ARRIVAL AND TRIAGE

      1.   Meet patient at transport vehicle after donning protective clothing

      2.   Assess ABC's: perform necessary life-saving measures. Follow instructions given by authorities.

      3.   Assess type of chemical/radioactive contamination (Radiation: See Lethal Dose, page A-23)
         a.   Whole or partial body exposure - no contaminant contact
            (1)   Exposure from an external source
            (2)   Patient is NOT a hazard to attendants
         b.   Internal contamination by inhalation or ingestion
            (1)   Contamination caused by airborne exposure
            (2)   Patient is NOT a hazard to attendants once clothing is removed and skin is decontaminated
         c.   External contamination of body surface
            (1)   Contamination by liquids or dirt
            (2)   Patient IS a hazard to attendants until decontaminated
         d.   External contamination complicated by wounds
            (1)   Patient IS a hazard to attendants until decontaminated
            (2)   Patient is considered to also have internal contamination

    **4.   Brief radiological survey performed with survey meter to determine if patient contaminated (See Table I - "How to Survey a Patient for Contamination," page A-19)
         a.   Done only if patient condition allows
         b.   Readings two (2) times above background determine possible contamination (TCGH background is .3 mR/hr.)
            (1)   Record findings (Use Anatomical Record Form, page A-10)
               (a)   Non-contaminated patients proceed for regular care
               (b)   Contaminated patients proceed with decontamination procedure

      5.   Responsibilities of transport crew
         a.   Remove patient's clothing in or near transport vehicle
            (1)   Wrap and/or cover patient with two (2) clean sheets or blankets
               (a)   Clothing should have been removed at incident scene if transported by ambulance
            (2)   Assist hospital staff with decontamination and/or placing on clean receiving stretcher.
            (3)   If patient positive for contamination, follow guidelines for care of contaminated material
               (a)   Place clothing in plastic bag-lined bio-medical waste container (label "CONTAMINATED")
               (b)   Place all contaminated materials (i.e., bedding, blood, urine, jewelry, dentures, belts) from the ambulance in plastic bag-lined bio-medical waste container (label "CONTAMINATED")
               (c)   Save for examination by appropriate authorities or by Radiation Safety Officer (RSO)
                  1)   DO NOT DISCARD

      6.   Transport crew to remain with vehicle until released by RSO

B.   DECONTAMINATION OF THE UNINJURED AND/OR NON-CRITICAL PATIENT

1.   Reassure and explain procedures to patients.

2.   Transfer patient to decontamination area (outdoors if possible).

3.   a.   Decontaminate outdoors if appropriate.
   b.   Survey or assess patient (use survey meter if radiological)
   c.   Document (Record results on Anatomical Record Form, page a-10.)
   **d.   Decontaminate if reading more than two (2) times background (TCGH background is .3 mR/hr.) (300 microrads/hr.)
      (1)   Avoid getting fluids in the ears, eyes, nose or mouth
      (2)   Hose patient down with lukewarm water - Resurvey - Document
         (a)   A shower may be used if feasible
         (b)   Use clean towels after each shower or hosing
         (c)   Place all materials used in a plastic bag lined bio-medical waste container (label "CONTAMINATED")
      **(d)   Survey after each shower - Document
   **(3)   Continue with progressive decontamination and patient treatment in the C/REA if survey readings remained unchanged after five (5) washings with water

4.   Proceed to C/REA
   a.   Assess level of consciousness and record vital signs
      (1)   Note allergies, medications
      (2)   Any history of illnesses
      (3)   Any recent nuclear medicine studies
      (4)   Complete physical exam
      (5)   Pregnant?
   b.   Collect appropriate samples
      (1)   Collect CBC with differential and UA for baseline (See Table II, pages A-20, 21)
         (a)   Cleanse area thoroughly before venipuncture with soap and water followed with alcohol or betadine
   **c.   External contamination monitoring
      (1)   Survey with survey meter - Document (Use Anatomical Record Form, page A-10)
         (a)   Mark areas of highest contamination with skin markers
      (2)   Moisten swabs with water and collect samples from body orifices, wounds, and skin
         (a)   Seal each swab in its own plastic container
         (b)   Label each swab with name, date, time, and site
      **(c)   Survey each swab and record findings
      **(d)   Bag and store swabs (label "Contaminated")
      **(e)   RSO will conduct final survey of swabs. Do not discard.

5.   Localize area of contamination with plastic sheet and/or drape. Tape to prevent further contamination.

6.   Decontaminate wounds and body orifices first and highest contaminated intact skin second (assume internal contamination if wound contaminated (See Internal Contamination, page A-16)
   a.   Open Wounds (AVOID CROSS-CONTAMINATION - Never dip cleansing instrument into cleaning agent, pour or shake)
      (1)   Chemical: Decontaminate as appropriate protecting other areas
   **(2)   Radiation:
      **(a)   Drape area with waterproof drapes and irrigate with saline, sterile water or Hydrogen peroxide

        **(b)   Blot dry, remove contaminated material (retain material for further survey

        **(c)   Resurvey - Document results on same Anatomical Record

        **(d)   If contamination level remains high after repeated cleansing, surgical debridement should be considered (retain tissue for assessment)

            **1)   Use fresh cleaning materials after each cleansing

            **2)   Change cleaning agents frequently if highly contaminated area

        **(e)   Cover decontaminated wounds with waterproof dressing

        **(f)   Continue with decontamination of other areas

        **(g)   Delay suturing until patient moved to a decontaminated area

   b.   Body Orifices

     (1)   Chemical: Decontaminate as appropriate

  **(2)   Radiation:

        **(a)   Brush teeth and rinse mouth with 3% citric acid solution (Bi-citra 15cc/H_2O 15cc - 3% solution)

        **(b)   Gargle with 3% Hydrogen peroxide for pharyngeal contamination

        **(c)   Rinse eyes and nose with tap water or saline

            **1)   Irrigate with copious amounts of water

            **2)   Change to normal saline as soon as possible

        **(d)   Treat irrigation induced conjunctivitis as usual

        **(e)   Survey irrigation fluid at frequent intervals and record results

     (3)   Irrigate ears with water or normal saline, using an ear syringe if tympanic membrane is intact

   c.   Contaminated Skin

     (1)   Chemical: Decontaminate as appropriate

  **(2)   Radiation:

        **(a)   Wash area gently under a stream of warm water while scrubbing with a soft brush or sponge

            **1)   Do not abrade skin or cause erythema

            **2)   Pat dry

            **3)   Resurvey - Document results on Anatomical Record (see page A-10)

            **4)   Proceed with more progressive cleaning if still contaminated

        **(b)   Progressive cleansing agents

            **1)   Mild soap or surgical scrub soap

            **2)   Sodium hypochlorite or household bleach

            **3)   Abrasive soap (i.e., Lava)

            **4)   3% Hydrogen peroxide solution

            **5)   Shampoo

        **(c)   Following removal of contamination, apply cream and cover area

        **(d)   Survey - Document results on same Anatomical Record (see page A-10)

            **1)   Record documentation following each cleansing

   d.   Internal Contamination

     (1)   Chemical: Decontaminate as appropriate

  **(2)   Radiation:

        **(a)   Secure appropriate samples (See Table II, pages A-20, 21)

        **(b)   Proceed with Internal Contamination antidote (See Table III, page A-22)

        **(c)   Patient admitted with an airway or ET tube is considered to be internally contaminated (no special equipment or procedures are needed for ventilator)

        **(d)   Save all body wastes for assessing amount of radio-active materials present

            **1)   Used to determine total radiation dose received

            **2)   Used to determine appropriate therapy

7.   Follow procedure for "Internal Contamination" for patients having inhalation or ingestion contamination

8. Transfer patient out of C/REA when contamination as low as possible and patient treated and stable
    a. See "Transfer of Patient From the Chemical/Radiation Emergency Area", page A-17

9. Place all materials used (i.e., drapes, dressings, linen, sharps containers, miscellaneous supplies, etc.) in plastic bag-lined bio-medical boxes (label "CONTAMINATED"). Do not discard sample.
    a. See "Decontamination of the Chemical/Radiological Emergency Response Team," page A-18)

10. Documentation (See "Documentation" requirements, page A-17)

C. DECONTAMINATION OF THE CRITICAL PATIENT (Life Threatening)
1. Perform life-saving functions

2. Transfer to clean, waterproof draped stretcher prior to entering facility and C/REA. Cover patient with clean sheets or blankets.

3. a. Decontamination in chemical/radiation Emergency Area
   b. Survey or assess as patient condition allows
   c. Document (Record results on Anatomical Record Form, page A-10)
   d. Decontaminate gross chemical contaminate as appropriate.
   **e. Decontaminate if background reading more than two (2) times background (TCGH background is .3 mR/hr.)

4. Proceed to C/REA
   a. Assess level of consciousness and record vital signs
      (1) Note allergies, medications
      (2) Any history of illnesses
      (3) Any recent nuclear medicine studies
      (4) Complete physical exam
      (5) Pregnant?
   b. Collect appropriate samples
      **(1) (Table II, pages A 20, 21) - Collect CBC with differential and UA for baseline
          (a) Cleanse area thoroughly before venipuncture with soap and water followed with alcohol or betadine
   **c. External contamination monitoring
      (1) Survey with survey meter - Document (use Anatomical Record Form, page A-10)
          (a) Mark areas of highest contamination with skin marker
      (2) Moisten swabs with water and collect samples from body orifices, wounds, and skin
          (a) Seal each swab in its own plastic container
          (b) Label each swab in its own plastic container
          **(c) Survey each swab and record findings
          **(d) Bag and store swabs (label "CONTAMINATED")
          **(e) RSO will conduct final survey of swabs. Do not discard.

5. Localize area of contamination with plastic sheet and/or drape, tape to prevent further contamination

6. Decontaminate wounds and body orifices first and highest contaminated intact skin second (assume internal contamination if wound contaminated (see Internal Contamination, page 14)
   a. Avoid getting fluids in the ears, eyes, nose or mouth
   b. Open Wounds (AVOID CROSS-CONTAMINATION - Never dip cleansing instrument into cleaning agent, pour or shake)

      (1) Chemical: Decontaminate as appropriate
    **(2) Radiation:
        **(a) Drape area with waterproof drapes and irrigate with saline, sterile water or Hydrogen peroxide.
        **(b) Blot dry, remove contaminated material (retain material for further survey)
        **(c) Resurvey - Document results on same Anatomical Record
        **(d) If contamination level remains high after repeated cleansing, surgical debridement should be considered. (Retain tissue for assessment)
            **1) Use fresh cleaning materials after each cleansing
            **2) Change cleaning agents frequently if highly contaminated area
        **(e) Cover decontaminated wounds with waterproof dressing
        **(f) Continue with decontamination of other areas
        **(g) Delay suturing until patient moved to a decontaminated area

c.   Body Orifices
      (1) Chemical: Decontaminate as appropriate
    **(2) Radiation:
        **(a) Brush teeth and rinse mouth with 3% citric acid solution (Bi-citra 30cc/H_2O - 30cc)
        **(b) Gargle with 3% Hydrogen peroxide for pharyngeal contamination
        **(c) Rinse eyes and nose with tap water or saline
             **1) Irrigate with copious amounts of water
            **2) Change to normal saline as soon as possible
        **(d) Treat irrigation induced conjunctivitis as usual
        **(e) Survey irrigation fluid at frequent intervals and record results
      (3) Irrigate ears with water or normal saline, using an ear syringe if tympanic membrane is intact

d.   Contaminated Skin
      (1) Chemical: Decontaminate as appropriate
    **(2) Radiation:
        **(a) Wash area gently under a stream of warm water while scrubbing with a soft brush or sponge
             **1) Do not abrade skin or cause erythema
             **2) Pat dry
             **3) Resurvey - Document results on Anatomical Record (see page A-10)
             **4) Proceed with more progressive cleaning if still contaminated
        **(b) Progressive cleansing agents
             **1) Mild soap or surgical scrub soap
             **2) Sodium hypochlorite or household bleach
             **3) Abrasive soap (i.e., Lava)
             **4) 3% Hydrogen peroxide solution
             **5) Shampoo
        **(c) Following removal of contamination, apply cream and cover area
        **(d) Survey - Document results on same Anatomical Record (see page A-10)
             1) Record documentation following each cleansing

e.   Internal Contamination
      (1) Chemical: Decontaminate as appropriate
    **(2) Radiation:
        **(a) Secure appropriate samples (See Table II, pages A-20, 21)
        **(b) Proceed with internal contamination antidote (See Table III, page A-22)
        **(c) Patient admitted with an airway or ET tube is considered to be internally contaminated (no special equipment or procedures are needed for ventilator)
        **(d) Save all body wastes for assessing amount of radioactive materials present
             **1) Used to determine total radiation dose received

2) Used to determine appropriate therapy

7. Follow procedure for "Internal Contamination" for patients having inhalation or ingestion contamination

8. Transfer patient out of C/REA when contamination as low as possible and patient treated and stable.
   a. See "Transfer of Patient from the Chemical/Radiation Emergency Area", page A-17)

9. Place all materials used (i.e., drapes, dressings, linen, sharps containers, miscellaneous supplies, etc.) in plastic bag-lined-bio-medical boxes (label "CONTAMINATED"). Do not discard.
   a. See "Decontamination of the Chemical/Radiological Emergency Response Team," pages A-18)

10. Documentation - See "Documentation" requirements, page A-17)

D. TRANSFER OF PATIENT FROM THE CHEMICAL/RADIATION EMERGENCY AREA
   1. Perform final complete body survey before discharge
      a. Thoroughly dry body
      **b. Reswab previous areas and again seal swabs in plastic
         **(1) Label swab with name, date, time, and site
         **(2) Survey and record finding
         **(3) Bag and store swabs (label "POST-CONTAMINATED")
         **(4) RSO performs final survey before discarding or saving.

   2. Lay clean floor covering to patient stretcher and bring in clean stretcher

   3. Clean attendants transfer to clean stretcher

   **4. RSO performs final survey of patient and stretcher (Special attention to wheels) with survey meter - Document

   5. Transfer patient to another location outside of the C/REA

E. CONTAMINATIONED CORPSES
   1. Contaminated corpses will be handled in accordance with state recommendations.

F. DOCUMENTATION
   1. Routine medical records and assessment including question regarding pregnancy.

   **2. Survey readings
      a. Anatomical Record Form (See page A-10)

   3. Samples taken and time

   4. Description of accident

   5. Effectiveness of decontamination

   6. Note pre-existing conditions, rashes, healing wounds, scars

VII. DECONTAMINATION OF THE CHEMICAL/RADIOLOGICAL EMERGENCY RESPONSE TEAM

NOTE: Chemical Emergency Response Team decontamination and exit procedures are same as radiological, except no monitoring, dosimeters, etc.

A. EXITING FROM THE CHEMICAL/RADIATION AREA (C/REA)
1. Each member goes to the control line and removes their protective clothing (one person designated to assist with removal and bagging)
    a. Remove outer gloves first, turning them inside out as they are pulled off
    b. Give Dosimeter to RSO for final reading (if dosimeters were available)
        (1) All practical efforts will be made to reduce personnel exposure to less than 100 mr
    c. Remove all tape at trouser cuffs and sleeves
    d. Remove outer surgical gown, turn inside out (avoid shaking)
    e. Pull surgical trousers off over shoe covers
    f. Remove head cover and mask
    g. Remove shoe cover from one foot and let RSO monitor shoe
        (1) If shoe is clean, step over control line
        (2) Remove other shoe cover and monitor other shoe
        (3) If either shoe contaminated, remove and replace with new shoe cover
    h. Remove inner gloves
    **i. Do total body radiological survey of each team member
        (1) Document and record
        (2) Decontaminate if readings greater than three (3) times background
        (3) Follow same procedure as "Decontamination of the Non-Injured Patient"
    j. Shower and shampoo with soap and water
    (1) If shower outside C/REA, these secondary showers are considered a control area
    k. Final survey
        (1) Personnel dressed in street clothes to report to the control point for a final survey
        (2) Document
    l. Secure and post sign(s) after all personnel exit control area(s)
        (1) Sign: "CAUTION - CHEMICAL/RADIATION AREA"
    **m. All involved personnel will be requested to collect three (3) successive 24-hour urine specimens for analysis of radioactivity

2. All materials removed to be placed in a plastic bag-lined bio-medical box and left in C/REA
    a. Label "CONTAMINATED"
    b. Leave one box near control line for last person

3. Area remains secured until checked and decontaminated by appropriate personnel: RSO or other health physics experts
    a. Radiation Safety Officer - Check with Radiology
    b. Department of Energy (DOE) (for this particular hospital, may be state Radiological Health Agency)

VIII. GENERAL INFORMATION

**A.   TABLE I - "HOW TO SURVEY A PATIENT FOR CONTAMINATION"

A patient survey can be done simultaneously with other emergency procedures, provided there is no interference with needed emergency care.

1.   Use a low-range survey meter, such as a CD V-700 (may be supplied by EMS or Fire Department. RSO will use the survey meter out of Nuclear Medicine.)

2.   Before entering the decontamination room or before patient arrival, perform operational check of instrument and determine background level; open the shield on the probe; cover the probe with a small plastic bag or plastic glove.

3.   Set instrument selector switch to the X 1 range (CD V-700) or most sensitive scale of the instrument.

4.   When necessary, adjust the range of the instrument by moving the selector switch. Meter readings should not be taken when the dial indicator reads in the lower 10 percent of the scale when on the X 100 and X 10 ranges. Turn the selector switch to the next most sensitive range to measure the exposure rate more accurately.

5.   Holding the probe approximately 1 inch from the patient's skin, systematically survey the entire body from head to toe on all sides. Move the probe slowly (about 1 inch per second) and pay particular attention to wounds, orifices, body folds, hairy areas and hands.

6.   An increase in count rate or exposure rate above background indicates the presence of radiation.

7.   Document time and radiation measurements on an anatomical drawing; each subsequent survey result should be documented.

8.   The use of headphones with the CD V-700 facilitates monitoring.

**B. TABLE II - RADIOLOGICAL AND CLINICAL LABORATORY ASSESSMENTS

All samples must be placed in separate, labeled containers that specify name, date, time of sampling, area of samples, and size of area samples. Medical, legal, and other postaccident investigations require that no blood, urine, feces, or other samples taken in the emergency treatment period be disposed of without authorization.

SAMPLES NEEDED	WHY?	HOW?
In all cases of radiation injury:		
CBC and differential STAT (follow with absolute lymphocyte counts every 6 hours for 48 hours when history indicates possibility of total-body irradiation)	To assess the radiation dose; initial counts establish a baseline, subsequent counts reflect the degree of injury	Choose a noncontaminated area for veni-puncture; cover puncture site after collection
Routine urinalysis	To determine if kidneys are functioning normally and establish a baseline of urinary constituents; especially important if internal contamination is a possibility	Avoid contaminating specimen during collection; if necessary, give the patient plastic gloves to wear for collection of specimen; label specimen "Number 1", with date and time
When external contamination is suspected:		
Swabs from body orifices	To assess possibility of internal contamination	Use separate saline- or water-moistened swabs to wipe the inner aspect of each nostril, each ear, mouth, etc.
Swabs from wounds	To determine if wounds are contaminated	Use moist or dry swabs to sample secretions from each wound, or collect a few drops of secretion from each using a dropper or syringe; for wounds with visible debris, use applicator or long tweezers or forceps to transfer samples to specimen containers which are placed in lead storage containers (pigs)
Skin wipes	To locate contaminated areas	Use filter paper, smear pads, or compresses to wipe sample areas 10cm x 10cm in size.
When internal contamination is suspected:		
Urine: 24-hour specimen x 4 days	Body excreta may contain radionuclides if internal contamination has occurred	Use 24-hour urine collection container

LEGEND: ** = Applies to Radiation only

**B. TABLE II (Continued)

Feces x 4 days	Body excreta may contain radionuclides if internal contamination has occurred	Save excreta in plastic containers in refrigerator or freezer
Vomitus	Body excreta may contain radionuclides if internal contamination has occurred	Save excreta in plastic containers in refrigerator or freezer
Sputum	To assess respiratory tract contamination if inhalation of contaminant was a possibility	Use a 5-percent propylene-glycol aerosol to get a deep cough specimen
Serum creatinine	To assess kidney function if chelation is indicated	Clinical chemistry

Other samples needed:

All irrigating fluids	Radiological assessment	Save in sealed and labeled, glass or plastic-lined containers

LEGEND: ** = Applies to Radiation only

An Orientation to Hazardous Materials for Medical Personnel

C. TABLE III - MEDICATIONS AND MECHANISMS OF DECORPORATION (MODIFIED FROM SAFETY SERIES 47, IAEA)

Radionuclide	Medication	Applications in Ingestion/Inhalation	Wound	Principle of Action
Iodine	KI	130 mg (tabl) stat, followed by 130 mg q.d. x 7 if indicated	Same	Blocking
Rare earths Plutonium Transplutonics Yttrium	DTPA	1 gm Ca-DTPA in 500 ml 5-percent D/W i.v. over 60 min; or 1 gm (4ml) in 6 ml 5-percent D/W by slow i.v. injection (1 min)	Irrigate wound with 1 gm of Ca-DTPA in 250 ml D5W	Chelation
Polonium Mercury Arsenic Bismuth Gold	BAL	One ampule (=300 mg) i.m. q4 hrs. for 3 days - (first test for sensitivity with ¼ amp.)	Same	Promotes excretion
Uranium	Bicarbonate	Slow i.v. infusion of bicarbonated physiological solution (250 ml at 14 percent)	Slow i.v. infusion of bicarbonated physiological solution (250 ml at 14 percent) and wash with bicarbonate	Alkalinization of urine; reduces chance of ATN
Cesium Rubidium Thallium	Prussian Blue* (Ferrihexacy ano-Ferrate (ll)	1 gm in 100-200 ml water p.o. t.i.d. for several days	Same	Mobilization from organs and tissues - reduction and absorption
Radium	Ca-gluconate	May be tried; 20-percent Cagluconate 10 ml ilv. Once or twice daily	Same	Displacement
Strontium	Ammonium chloride	3 gm t.i.d. p.o.	Same	Demineralizing agent
Tritium	Water	Hae patient drink 6-12 literse of water per day	Same	Isotopic dilution
Strontium Radium	BaSO$_4$	100 gm BaSO$_4$ in 250 ml of water	Same	Reduces absorption
Calcium Barium	Sodium alginate	10 gm in a large glass of water	Same	Inhibits absorption
Copper Polonium Lead Mercury Gold	D-Penicilla-mine	1 gm i.v. q.d. or 0.9 gm p.o. 4-6 hours	Same	Chelation

*Not FDA approved as of publication date

LEGEND: ** = Applies to Radiation only

D. LETHAL DOSE AND ACUTE RADIATION SYNDROME

1. LETHAL DOSE (L.D.)
    a. May occur in patient who has received full or partial body external radiation exposure
        (1) L.D. 100 in man approximately 800 REM
        (2) L.D. 50 in man approximately 400 REM
            (a) Definition of L.D. 50 - dose which will produce an acute illness (A.R.S.) followed by death in 30-60 days in 50% of the people thus exposed.
        (3) Triage will be necessary if widespread accident, such as in a major nuclear disaster or war attack to segregate patients and keep those exposed to an L.D. 100 comfortable, but save supplies and manpower for persons in which there is some hope for recovery.
        (4) Lower doses (L.D. 30, L.D. 10)
            (a) Effect of lower dose is proportionately less
                1) At 100 REM only 15% of people develop any symptoms
                2) At 25-50 REM no clinical findings are present and the syndrome is only diagnosable by laboratory tests (blood count changes)

2. ACUTE RADIATION SYNDROME (A.R.S.)
    a. Assume a dose of 400 REM (L.D. 50). This dose almost invariably would be from external radiation
    b. Smaller doses would show an attenuated A.R.S. both in time and severity of symptoms
        (1) Early Phase (1 hour to 2 days)
            (a) Nausea plus or minus vomiting
            (b) Malaise plus or minus hyperexcitability of reflexes
        (2) Asymptomatic Phase (2 hours to 2 days)
            (a) Patient feels well but tissue damage is progressing
                1) WBC drops during first day; first lymphocytes, then granulocytes to the range of 1000 cells per cc.
                2) RBCs and platelets follow in dropping
            (b) Internal bleeding
                1) G.I.
                2) Skin
        (3) Height of Disease (2 to 3 weeks)
            (a) Elevated temperature in the range of 103-104 degrees
            (b) Exhaustion
            (c) Weight loss
            (d) Reddened skin
            (e) Loss of hair
            (f) Hemorrhages in skin
            (g) Ulcerated mucous membrane
            (h) G.I. hemorrhages
            (i) Infection, may be ultimate cause of death
            (j) Fluid imbalance
        (4) Delayed effects in survivors
            (a) Hair loss
            (b) Cataracts
            (c) Anemia
            (d) Leukopenia, may go on to Leukemia
            (e) Impaired spermatogenesis
            (f) Premature aging, shortens life span

E. CHEMICAL/RADIOACTIVE WASTE DISPOSAL
1. CONTAMINATED WASTE (body substances/secretions, water and other liquids)
   a. Flush into ordinary floor drains and sinks
      (1) Leave faucets turned on to ensure adequate dilution
   b. Wash into outside storm drains
      (1) Leave hose running to wash contaminants into drains
      (2) Be careful not to splash

2. CONTAMINATED DISPOSABLE SUPPLIES
   a. Place in plastic bag-lined bio-medical waste containers
   b. Label "CONTAMINATED - RADIOACTIVE"
   c. Leave for proper disposal by appropriate personnel
      (1) RSO or his/her designee
      (2) Department of Energy (DOE)

3. CONTAMINATED EQUIPMENT
   a. Equipment will remain in the Chemical/Radioactive Emergency Area (C/REA) until decontaminated or removed by appropriate personnel
      (1) RSO or his/her designee
      (2) DOE or State Radiological Health

**F. RADIOLOGICAL SURVEY OF INSTRUMENTS
1. RADIOLOGICAL SURVEY EQUIPMENT INSPECTION
   a. Survey and Dosimeter meters will be inspected and calibrated once a week
      (1) Radiology responsible for the Ludlum survey meter
         (a) Tested weekly and after daily nuclear usage
      (2) EMS and/or County Fire Department responsible for their own CD V-700 survey meters
      (3) Dosimetry system not in place at present
   b. Operational check for the Ludlum survey meter
      (1) Observe battery strength on meter face
      (2) Check audio (Listen for sound)
      (3) Read background readings
         (a) Meter set on 0.1 mR/hr
      (4) Verify accuracy using Cs137 check source (.99mCl)
   c. Operational check for the CD V-700 survey meters (if available)
      (1) Install fresh batteries
         (a) Observe the indicated polarity
      (2) Turn selector switch to the 10 range
      (3) Allow 30 seconds for warm-up time
      (4) Open the probe shield and place the open area directly against the check source
         (a) Needle should move to mid-range (1.5-2.5 mr/hr.)
      (5) Determine the background radiation level
         (a) Set instrument on X-1
         (b) Observe reading for 30 seconds (if fluctuates, average readings)
      (6) Note findings
      (7) Remove batteries and return to storage box (when situation is over)
   d. Operational check for a Dosimeter-Charger

**G. HALF-LIFE OF SELECTED ISOTOPES

Name	Radiation	Symbol	Half-Life	Critical Organ
Americium 241	alpha, gamma	Am241	458 years	bone
Barium 140	beta, gamma	Ba140	12.8 days	bone
Cadium 109	gamma	Cd109	13 days	bone
Calcium 45	beta	Ca45	453 days	liver
Calcium 47	beta, gamma	Ca47	165 days	bone
Carbon 14	beta	C14	5,730 years	total body
Cesium 137	beta, gamma	Ce137	30 years	total body
Chromium 51	gamma	Cr51	28 days	total body
Cobalt 57	gamma	Co57	270 days	total body
Cobalt 60	beta, gamma	Co60	5.3 years	total body
Europium 152	beta, gamma	Eu152	13 years	kidney
Fluorine 18	beta, gamma	F18	2 hours	total body
Gold 198	beta, gamma	Au198	2.7 days	total body
Hydrogen 3 (Tritium)	beta	II3	12 years	total body
Iodine 125	beta, gamma	II25	60 days	thyroid
Iodine 131	beta, gamma	II31	8 days	thyroid
Iodine 132	beta, gamma	II32	2.3 hours	thyroid
Iodine 133	beta, gamma	II33	20.8 hours	thyroid
Iodine 134	beta, gamma	II34	52.5 minutes	thyroid
Iodine 135	beta, gamma	II35	6.7 hours	thyroid
Iron 55	beta, gamma	Fe55	2.6 years	spleen
Lead 210	beta, gamma	Pb210	20 years	kidney
Mercury 197	gamma	Hg197	3 days	kidney
Molybdenum 99	beta, gamma	Mo99	3 days	kidney
Neptunium 239	beta, gamma	Np239	2 days	GE tract
Phosphorus 32	beta	P32	14 days	bone
Polonium 210	alpha	Po210	138 days	spleen
Potassium 32	beta, gamma	K32	12 hours	total body
Promethium 149	beta, gamma	Pm149	2 days	bone
Radium 224	alpha, gamma	Ra224	4 days	bone
Radium 226	alpha, gamma	Ra226	1,600 years	bone
Rubidium 86	beta, gamma	Rb86	19 days	total body
Ruthenium 106	beta	Ru106	368 days	kidney
Sodium 22	beta, gamma	Na22	2.6 years	total body
Strontium 85	gamma	Sr85	65 days	total body
Strontium 90	beta	Sr90	28 days	bone
Technetium 99	beta	Tc99	2E5 years	kidney
Technetium 99m	beta	Tc99m	6 hours	kidney
Thorium 230	alpha, gamma	Th230	8E4 years	bone
Thorium Natural	alpha, beta, gamma	Th	1.4E10 years	bone
Uranium 238	alpha, gamma	U238	4.5E9 years (x10^9)	kidney
Uranium Natural	alpha, beta, gamma	U	4.5E9 years	kidney
Zinc 65	beta, gamma	Zn65	245 days	total body
Zirconium 95	beta, gamma	Zr95	66 days	total body

Source: Radiation and Health: Principles and Practice in Therapy and Disaster Preparedness. Aspen, 1984.

LEGEND: ** = Applies to Radiation only

APPENDIX B: ANSWER KEYS

ANSWER KEY: UNIT 1: POST-TEST

Directions: Answer each of the following questions. Each item counts 25 points. When you finish, check your answers in Appendix B. If you missed any items, refer to the applicable sections before you proceed.

1. Identify three ways in which hospitals may be involved in hazardous materials incidents.

   Any of the following answers is acceptable:

   Patients exposed or contaminated may arrive at the emergency department.

   The facility may be in the path of exposure of the release and may have to institute protective procedures.

   The facility may have to be evacuated.

   Hospitals will have to diagnose hazardous materials and determine the appropriate treatment.

2. Define hazardous materials.

   Hazardous materials are chemical substances that, if released or misused, can pose a threat to the environment, life or health.

3. List four federal regulations, standards, or agencies that regulate hazardous materials.

   Any of the following answers is acceptable:

   Code of Federal Regulations, SARA, OSHA, TSCA, Federal-agency issued regulations, standards and guidelines

4. Describe some of the health effects associated with hazardous materials.

   Heart ailments, kidney and lung damage, sterility, cancer, burns and rashes.

Appendix B: Answer Keys

Appendix B: Answer Keys

ANSWER KEY: UNIT 2: PRETEST

PART I

1. Match the DOT hazardous materials classifications with the correct description. (Each answer counts 10 points.)

DOT Hazardous Materials Classification	Description
__D__ 1. Corrosive Materials	a. A chemical that causes a sudden, almost instantaneous release of pressure, gas and heat when subjected to sudden shock, pressure, or high temperatures.
__E__ 2. Radioactive Materials	b. Solids likely to cause fires through friction or retained heat from manufacturing or processing or that are easy to ignite such as matches.
__B__ 3. Flammable Solids	c. Materials that readily yield oxygen to support combustion.
__C__ 4. Oxidizers	d. Liquids or solids that damage human tissue or steel on contact such as sulfuric acid.
__A__ 5. Explosives	e. Substances that emit alpha and beta particles and gamma rays spontaneously.

PART II

2. List four potential causes for mechanisms of harm from hazardous materials. (Each answer counts five points.)

    Any of the following answers is correct:
    Thermal   Etiologic   Asphyxiant   Mechanical   Chemical   Psychological   Radiological

3. List six sources of potential hazardous materials within the home, work facility, and community. (Each answer counts 5 points.)

    Any of the following is acceptable:

    Transportation incidents   *Fixed facilities and storage*
    Automobiles   *Hazardous materials waste sites*
    Medical procedures   *Consumer products*
    Naturally occurring toxic substances   *Soil*
    Air   *Ground and Surface Water*

✓ Exercise: Identifying Mechanisms of Harm Effects on the Body (Unit 2)

ANSWER KEY

All of the systems would be affected, except for psychological. In this situation, it would only apply to the neurological, respiratory, circulatory and digestive systems.

Appendix B: Answer Keys

ANSWER KEY: UNIT 2: POST-TEST

PART I

Match the DOT hazardous classes with the appropriate description. (Each answer counts 10 points.)

DOT Hazardous Class	Description
__D__ 1. Flammable Gas	a. Anthrax, botulism, and polio virus
__E__ 2. Flammable Liquid	b. Flammable compounds that contain the double oxygen or peroxy group that are subject to explosive decomposition.
__B__ 3. Organic Peroxide	c. Matches or sulfur.
__A__ 4. Etiologic or Infectious Organism	d. Propane, methane, and hydrogen.
__C__ 5. Flammable Solid	e. Liquids with a flashpoint below 100 degrees F.

PART II

Match the potential mechanisms for harm according to their causes. Each answer counts 10 points.

Cause	Potential Harm
__B__ 1. Etiologic	a. Fireworks explode unexpectedly causing burns over 30 percent of the body.
__E__ 2. Asphyxiant	b. You are exposed to hepatitis on your visit to Malaysia.
__C__ 3. Radiological	c. Your basement contains excessive amounts of radon.
__D__ 4. Chemical	d. You spill nitric acid and it splashes into your eyes.
__A__ 5. Thermal	e. Your gas heater malfunctions and emits dangerous levels of carbon monoxide.

Appendix B: Answer Keys

ANSWER KEY: UNIT 3: PRETEST

1. What is the purpose of a hospital emergency/disaster response plan?

    The hospital emergency/disaster plan describes the policies and procedures that should be followed in the event of a hazardous materials incident.

2. List five individuals or agencies that should be involved in the development of a hospital's emergency/disaster response plan.

    Any of the following individuals or agencies would be acceptable answers:

    - *Medical staff*
    - *Nursing administrator*
    - *Facility engineer*
    - *Housekeeping services representative*
    - *Food service administrator*
    - *Emergency department administrator*
    - *Security officers*
    - *Risk management advisor*
    - *Public affairs representative*
    - *Communications representative*
    - *Safety director*
    - *Senior management representatives*
    - *Field Emergency Medical Service providers*
    - *Fire and law enforcement officials*
    - *Representatives of the Local Emergency Planning Committee*
    - *Red Cross and human service agencies*
    - *Hazardous materials response teams*
    - *911 and emergency dispatch centers*
    - *Poison Control Centers*
    - *Air ambulance services*
    - *Other hospital and medical centers*
    - *Public health agencies*
    - *Visiting Nurse Associations*
    - *Emergency Management Agency*

ANSWER KEY: UNIT 3: PRETEST (continued)

3. List five basic elements that should be included in the hospital's emergency/disaster response plan.

    Any five of the following would be acceptable:

    - *Roles and Responsibilities of the Hospital and Staff*
    - *Organizational and Reporting Structure in an Emergency*
    - *Fire Plan*
    - *Procedures and Policies for Access to Emergency Care Areas*
    - *Communications Systems Alternatives (when main communication system fails)*
    - *Procedures to follow when Electrical, Air Conditioning, Plumbing, Boiler Systems, and Essential Life Support Systems fail*
    - *Procedures for Patient Management (scheduling, modification, discontinuation of services, control of patient information, and admission, transfer, and discharge of patients)*
    - *Evacuation Plan*
    - *Special Equipment Requirements (for Hazardous Materials Incidents)*

4. Why is it important to have a hospital emergency/disaster response plan?

    A hospital emergency/disaster response plan ensures that the facility is prepared to handle the expected and unexpected situations and needs that may occur during hazardous materials events.

5. What is the name or title of the individual who is responsible for the overall development of your hospital's emergency/disaster response plan?

    Your answers will vary.

Appendix B: Answer Keys

 Exercise: Interpreting the Hospital Emergency/Disaster Response Plan (Unit 3)
ANSWER KEY

Purpose: To become acquainted with a hospital emergency/disaster response plan.

Directions: Use your hospital's emergency/disaster response plan to answer the following questions. If you do not have a plan, use the sample plan in Appendix A.

1. Locate the section that identifies the personnel for response duties.
   Section III—Chemical/Radiation Hazards Response Team

2. Locate the section that defines the roles and responsibilities of personnel.
   Section II—Notification and Verification Responsibilities and
   Section III—Chemical/Radiation Hazards Response Team

3. Locate the section(s) that identifies the primary and secondary areas for patient reception triage and decontamination treatment.
   Section IV—Preparation of Chemical/Radiation Emergency Area (C/REA)

4. Locate the section(s) that identifies safety and security precautions that should be followed.
   Section IV—Preparation of Chemical/Radiation Emergency Area (C/REA) and
   Section V—Preparation of Chemical/Radiological Emergency Response Team

5. Locate the section(s) that identifies procedures for facility and personnel contamination control.
   Section IV—Preparation of Chemical/Radiation Emergency Area (C/REA) and
   Section VII—Decontamination of the Chemical/Radiological Emergency Response Team

   Note: Your answers will vary if you use your hospital's plan.

ANSWER KEY: UNIT 3: POST-TEST

Directions: Answer each of the questions below.

(Check your answers in Appendix B. If you missed any items, you should review this unit before proceeding).

(1) Which of the following documents would contain the policies and procedures that **you** should follow in your facility in responding to a hazardous materials incident?

    a) JCAHO Accreditation Manual for Hospitals
    b) Your hospital's emergency/disaster response plan
    c) The state's code of regulations
    d) The community emergency preparedness plan

(2) Which of the following is not a basic component of the hospital's emergency/disaster response plan?

    a) Basic plan
    b) Supporting annexes
    c) Implementing procedures
    d) **Community fire and building codes**

(3) Who should be involved in the development of the hospital's emergency/disaster response plan?

    a) Only management representatives from each department in the hospital
    b) All employees, including management and representatives from every department who may be involved in responding to a hazardous materials incident
    c) Just emergency physicians and nurses
    d) Primarily, the hospital administrator and security personnel

(4) What is the purpose of the hospital's emergency/disaster response plan?

    a) To provide details on how to control the spread of fires in the event of an emergency
    b) To provide job descriptions for hospital personnel
    c) To describe the policies and procedures to follow in the event of a hazardous materials incident.
    d) To identify the community's fire and sanitation ordinances

---

Appendix B: Answer Keys

ANSWER KEY: UNIT 4: PRETEST

Purpose: This pretest will assess your knowledge about issues and procedures in responding to hazardous materials incidents.

Directions: Read each item and answer accordingly. Each answer counts 20 points. *(If you score at or above the passing range of 85%, skip this unit and proceed to unit five. Do not check the Answer Key (Appendix B) until after you have completed the test.)*

1. When someone or something else comes in contact with someone or something else that has been contaminated, this is known as:
    a) **cross contamination**
    b) direct contamination
    c) residual contamination
    d) gross contamination

2. Removing a major amount but not all of the contaminant from the contaminated person or object is an example of:
    a) secondary decontamination
    b) **gross decontamination**
    c) full-stage decontamination
    d) level A decontamination

3. Chemical alteration of a hazardous material into a harmless substance is called _____.
    a) dilution
    b) **degradation**
    c) disinfection
    d) absorption

4. Which of the following is not a technique for contamination control?
    a) Monitor anyone or anything that leaves the controlled area.
    b) Control ventilation.
    c) Set up a controlled area large enough to hold the anticipated number of victims.
    d) **Register all victims at the reception desk before sending them to the decontamination area.**

5. List five members of the emergency response team.
    Any of the following is acceptable:
    Team coordinator, emergency physician, triage officer, nurse, technical recorder, safety officer, public information officer, administrator, security personnel, maintenance personnel, laboratory technician

---

Exercise: Who's Responsible for What? (Unit 4)

ANSWER KEY

Role Description	Team Member
__C__ 1. Secures the emergency area and controls crowds	a. Emergency Physician
__D__ 2. Leads, advises, coordinates	b. Public Information Officer
__A__ 3. Diagnoses, treats, and provides emergency medical care	c. Security Officer
__E__ 4. Records and documents medical, hazardous material, and radiological data	d. Team Coordinator
__B__ 5. Releases information to the media	e. Technical Recorder

Exercise: What's the Appropriate Method To Control the Spread of Hazardous Materials? (Unit 4)

ANSWER KEY

1. A wounded patient walks into the reception area. The patient says he just provided assistance at a hazardous materials accident, but was injured when some kind of chemical exploded. What should you do?

   (a) Assume the patient is contaminated and immediately direct him or her back outside.
   (b) Fill out the patient's information and insurance forms.
   (c) Ask the patient to describe the type of accident he was providing assistance.
   (d) Tell the patient to wait for the next available doctor.

2. You have been notified that you will be receiving 10 patients who have been exposed to some type of corrosive. What should you do first?

   (a) Prepare the emergency area.
   (b) Contact the security officer to control the crowds.
   (c) Notify the public relations officer.
   (d) Call the hazardous materials hotline.

3. Which of the following will not help to prevent the spread of contamination in a hospital?

   (a) Failure to close the air ventilation ducts in the emergency area.
   (b) Establishing a control zone for the decontamination area.
   (c) Setting up a warm zone between the contaminated and non-contaminated area.
   (d) Using strict isolation precautions including protective clothing.

Exercise: Why Do I Need a Sample? (Unit 4)

ANSWER KEY

Sample	Reason Required
__E__ 1. Routine urinalysis	a. In accidents involving radiation, to assess the radiation dose and establish a baseline
__C__ 2. Swabs from wounds	b. To assess respiratory tract contamination if inhalation of contaminant was a possibility
__B__ 3. Sputum	c. To determine if wounds are contaminated
__D__ 4. Serum creatinine	d. To assess kidney function if chelation is indicated
__A__ 5. Complete Blood Count	e. To determine if kidneys are functioning normally

Exercise: What Do You Know About Mechanisms for Decontamination? (Unit 4)
ANSWER KEY

Description	Term
__D__ 1. Process that neutralizes, degrades, or otherwise chemically alters the contaminant.	a. Absorption
__E__ 2. Destroys microorganisms and their toxins.	b. Dilution
__A__ 3. Penetration of liquid or gas into another substance.	c. Disposal
__C__ 4. Used more often to deal with contaminated clothing.	d. Degradation
__B__ 5. Reduces the concentration of the contaminant.	e. Disinfection

---

ANSWER KEY: UNIT 4: POST-TEST

1. When notified of a hazardous materials incident and the possible transport of patients, what should you do?

   a) **Get accurate and complete information from the person reporting the incident.**
   b) Call the local emergency management office to coordinate patient treatment.
   c) Notify the American Red Cross.
   d) Wait until the patients arrive before taking any action.

2. When a substance actually touches a body or thing, it is called

   a) Cross contamination
   b) Decontamination
   c) **Direct or primary contamination**
   d) Contaminated

3. Which of the following statements is not a characteristic of the emergency response team (ERT)?

   a) The composition of the ERT may vary from facility to facility.
   b) The hospital ERT must coordinate its efforts with field emergency response teams and other external agencies.
   c) The composition of the team, and the numbers of people needed will vary according to the magnitude of the situation.
   d) **The ERT consists of a limited number of people, usually the triage officer, nurse, and emergency physician.**

4. It is important to prepare an emergency area when dealing with hazardous materials incidents because:

   a) **Special preparation techniques protect the attending staff, hospital facility, and equipment while preventing the spread of contamination.**
   b) It will be easier for family members to see the patient.
   c) Doctors and nurses prefer to work in separate areas.
   d) It allows for continuous traffic flow and visitor movement within the area.

5. Protocol for "dirty" surgical cases is similar to the techniques applied in:

   a) Treating ill patients
   b) **Isolation of contaminated patients**
   c) Diagnosing wounded patients
   d) Triage

ANSWER KEY: UNIT 4: POST-TEST (continued)

6. To prepare a room for decontamination, you should:

   a) **Turn off the ventilation system.**
   b) Cover the movable equipment.
   c) Set up an open access area
   d) Avoid using control lines or control zones

7. Personal protection equipment should only be used when

   a) **Personnel have been trained in the OSHA requirements regarding its use**
   b) Poisonous vapors are present
   c) Instructed to do so by the ERT coordinator
   d) You perceive a danger

8. In dealing with hazardous materials incidents during patient assessment and triage

   a) You should follow routine procedures in all situations
   b) **You should care for noncontaminated patients like any other emergency case**
   c) You should take all patients to a decontamination area
   d) You should wait until you have details on the nature of the hazard before doing anything

9. Which of the following is **not** a reason you perform radiological and clinical laboratory assessments:

   a) To assess the biological effects
   b) **To identify abnormalities**
   c) To quantify radionuclide contamination, if exposed to radiation
   d) To aid in the detection of the hazard

10. When you perform gross decontamination, you

   a) **Remove or alter chemically the majority of the contaminant**
   b) Remove all traces of the contaminant
   c) Ensure that cross contamination does not occur
   d) Create potential hazards

ANSWER KEY: UNIT 5: PRETEST

Directions: Answer each question. Each answer counts 20 points. After you have completed the test, check your answers in Appendix B.

1. Can incorporation occur without contamination? Explain your answer.

   No, you must be contaminated before incorporation occurs, because some part of your body must come in contact with a hazardous material.

2. What are the three most common types of ionizing radiation?

   Alpha, beta, and gamma rays

3. What is the most penetrating type of ionizing radiation?

   Gamma rays

4. List two units of quantity of measuring radioactivity.

   Curie and Becquerel

5. List three elements of radiation protection.

   Time, Distance and Shielding

Exercise: Identifying Types of Radiation Injuries (Unit 5)

ANSWER KEY

Purpose: To assess your understanding of the types of radiation injuries.

Directions: Answer each question. You can check your answers in Appendix B. If you missed any, review this section before continuing.

---

1. Mary had a series of x-rays taken during her visit to the emergency room. What type of radiation exposure did she receive?

   External irradiation

2. Jim spilled a radioactive material on his skin. Is Jim contaminated or exposed or both?

   Jim would be both contaminated with radioactive material, and exposed to radiation.

3. Three school children accidentally picked up an unbroken, sealed container that had dropped off a truck that was carrying radioactive materials. Is it possible that they could experience incorporation? Why or why not?

   No, it is unbroken and sealed; there is no release of radioactive materials. The only hazard would be exposure.

Exercise: How Well Do You Know Your Physics? (Unit 5)

ANSWER KEY

Purpose: To assess your understanding of basic radiation physics.

Directions: Answer each item. Check your answers in Appendix B. If you missed any items, review this section before continuing on to the next section.

1. How do unstable atoms become stable?

   By emitting radiation.

2. Which type of ionizing radiation is the least penetrating?

   Alpha particles

3. What is the SI unit that measures the amount of radioactivity?

   Becquerel

4. What is the unit for radiation absorbed dose in SI units?

   Gray

5. What are two biological-effects units of absorbed radiation?

   Sievert and Rem

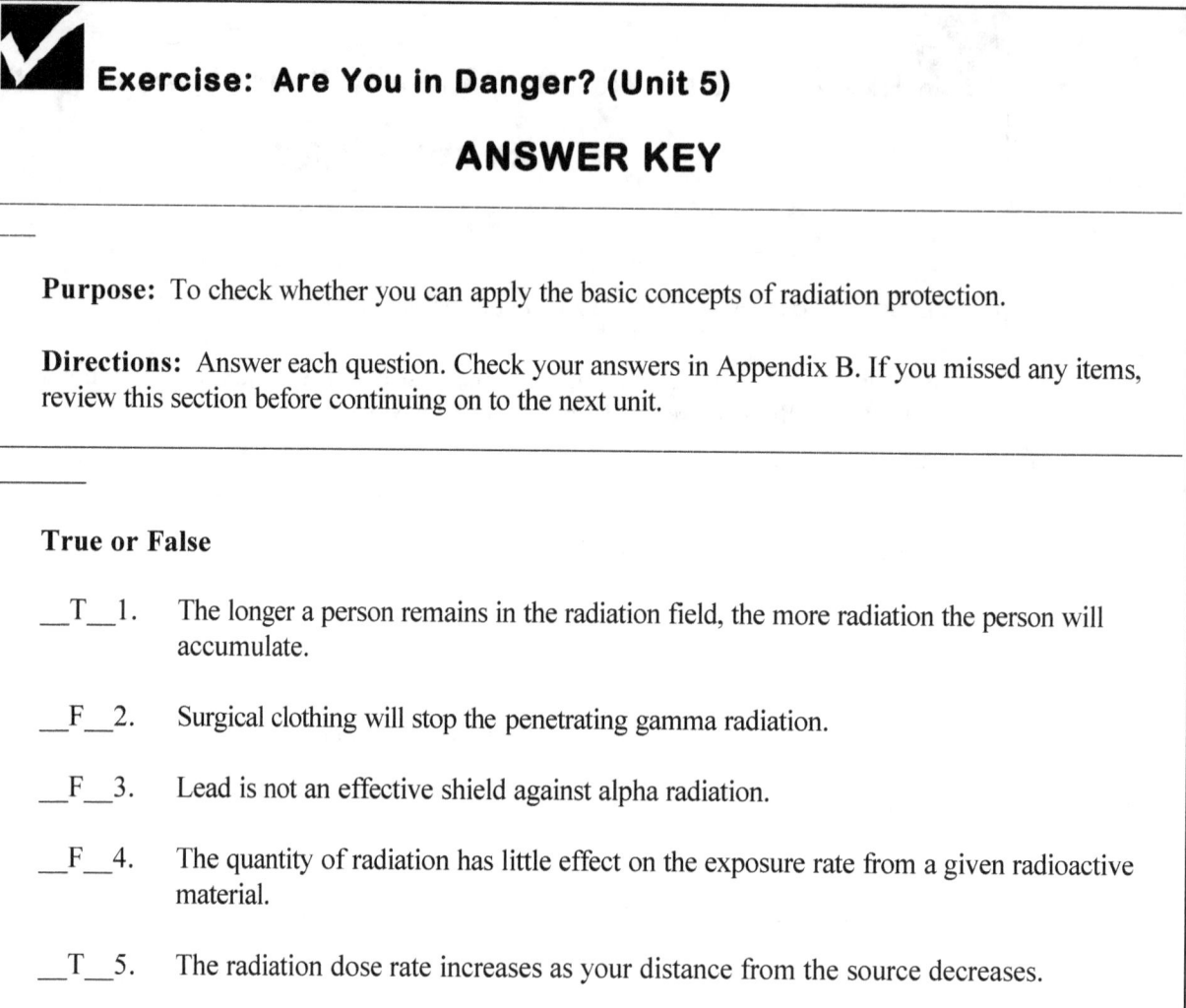

Exercise: Are You in Danger? (Unit 5)

ANSWER KEY

Purpose: To check whether you can apply the basic concepts of radiation protection.

Directions: Answer each question. Check your answers in Appendix B. If you missed any items, review this section before continuing on to the next unit.

True or False

__T__ 1. The longer a person remains in the radiation field, the more radiation the person will accumulate.

__F__ 2. Surgical clothing will stop the penetrating gamma radiation.

__F__ 3. Lead is not an effective shield against alpha radiation.

__F__ 4. The quantity of radiation has little effect on the exposure rate from a given radioactive material.

__T__ 5. The radiation dose rate increases as your distance from the source decreases.

ANSWER KEY: UNIT 5: POST-TEST

Directions: Answer each question. Each answer counts 10 points. Check your answers in Appendix B. If you missed any items, review this unit before taking the final examination.

---

1. John used a survey meter to measure the amount of radiation present and found none. Later, Sue used a different same meter and found significant amounts of radiation. What could have caused the differences in the readings?

   a) **John's meter was not working properly.**

   b) Radiation had time to register in the body because of the time that passed between the two readings.

   c) **Sue's body or clothing were contaminated with radioactive material.**

   d) **John did not use the proper type of meter to detect the type of radiation being emitted.**

2. Which of the following would expose you to the highest dose of radiation?

   a) Chest X-rays

   b) **Gamma rays**

   c) Beta particles

   d) Alpha particles

3. Which of the following is the highest source of radiation (on an annual basis)?

   a) Living in Chicago

   b) X-rays and nuclear medicine

   c) Living near a nuclear power plant

   d) **Radon in an average household**

4. What is the largest source of man-made radiation?

   a) **Radiation used in medicine**

   b) Nuclear power plants

   c) Scientific research

   d) Mining

ANSWER KEY: UNIT 5: POST-TEST (continued)

5. Which of the following takes priority in the treatment?
   a) Nausea and vomiting caused by exposure to 15 Gy external irradiation
   b) **Tension pneumothorax**
   c) Superficial leg laceration
   d) Decontamination

6. Which of the following particles pose an external and internal hazard?
   a) Beta particles
   b) Alpha particles
   c) **Beta and gamma particles**
   d) Alpha and beta particles

7. The rad, rem, and gray are measures of what?
   a) **Absorbed dose**
   b) Units of exposure
   c) Amount of radioactivity
   d) Degrees of radiation

8. An important goal of emergency responders in dealing with radiation-related incidents should be to:
   a) **Protect the public**
   b) Save lives at any cost
   c) **Keep their own radiation exposure ALARA**
   d) **Treat all patients as emergency care victims**

9. What is the EPA recommended maximum dose for any single life-threatening emergency?
   a) 5
   b) 10
   c) **25**
   d) 50

10. What happens at the fourth stage in acute radiation syndrome?
    a) **Recovery or death**
    b) Nausea and diarrhea
    c) Weakness
    d) Gastrointestinal syndrome

ANSWER KEY: UNIT 6: FINAL EVALUATION

1. Which of the following statements best describes a hospital's involvement in hazardous materials and events?
    a) Hospitals are seldom involved in hazardous materials incidents.
    b) A hospital's primary purpose is to help diagnose the nature of the hazardous chemical.
    c) A hospital's involvement primarily centers on the decontamination of patients.
    d) A hospital's involvement in hazardous materials incidents may take many forms, including diagnosis of the hazardous material and treatment of contaminated patients.

2. Which of the following groups designates compliance issues regarding hazardous materials?
    a) State and local transportation agencies
    b) The Joint Commission for the Accreditation of Hospitals
    c) EPA, NRC, and OSHAEPA, NRC, and OSHA
    d) FBI, DOT, FEMA

3. A chemical that causes a sudden, almost instantaneous release of pressure, gas and heat when subjected to sudden shock, pressure or high temperatures best describes which type of DOT hazardous materials classification?
    a) Class 2—Gases
    b) Class 1—Explosives
    c) Class 6—Toxic (poisonous) materials and infectious substances
    d) Class 7—Radioactive materials

4. What type of injury is not likely to occur from a chemical?
    a) Bone damage
    b) Severe and deep tissue burns
    c) Eye damage
    d) Laceration or puncture to the skin

5. Which of the following is most likely to be a source of hazardous materials within the home?
    a) Recycled garbage
    b) Household cleaning products
    c) Heating pad
    d) Lawnmower

6. What is the purpose of a hospital emergency/disaster response plan?
    a) It describes the policies and procedures that should be followed in the event of a hazardous materials incident.
    b) It's a reference tool for external responders to an emergency.
    c) It ensures that the hospital is in compliance with OSHA regulations.
    d) It's a training tool for hospital personnel.

ANSWER KEY: UNIT 6: FINAL EVALUATION (continued)

7. Which of the following statements best describes the procedure that should be followed by the person first responding to a hazardous materials emergency call?
   a) Refer the call to the safety officer.
   b) Contact the security officer immediately.
   c) Assume the victim(s) are contaminated until proven otherwise and base any actions on that assumption.
   d) Notify the hospital's admission office of potential patients' arrival.

8. Under what circumstances is isolation necessary when dealing with hazardous materials events?
   a) When radioactive contamination is suspected
   b) When hazardous materials emit vapors or gases
   c) When hazardous materials contamination is known or suspected.
   d) During the hospital evacuation

9. What is the purpose of a control zone?
   a) To establish an area for the reception of contaminated patients
   b) To differentiate the controlled (contaminated) area from the noncontrolled (uncontaminated) are
   c) To control the flow of traffic into the hospital
   d) To set up barriers to prevent the media's access

10. When should you use Level C personal protection equipment?
    a) When the highest level of respiratory, skin, eye, and mucous membrane protection is needed
    b) When only minimal skin protection is required
    c) When you don't need much skin and eye protection
    d) When you don't require a high level of respiratory protection

11. Under what conditions would you take samples of vomitus, sputum and serum creatinine?
    a) When external contamination is suspected
    b) When internal contamination is suspected
    c) When you need to locate contaminated areas
    d) When there is the possibility of a lawsuit for incorrect actions

12. What is gross decontamination?
    a) Cross-contamination
    b) A type of secondary decontamination
    c) A lethal contaminant
    d) The removal or chemical alteration of the majority of a contaminant

13. If you remove the biological (etiologic) contamination hazards through destroying microorganisms and their toxins, what mechanism of decontamination did you use?
    a) Emulsification
    b) Disposal
    c) Disinfection

d) Absorption

ANSWER KEY: UNIT 6: FINAL EVALUATION (continued)

14. What is the name of a reference tool that is produced by chemical manufacturers that provides information on the chemical identify of the hazardous material, its known acute and chronic effects, and exposure limits, among other things?
    a) The Emergency Response Guidebook for Selected Hazardous Materials
    b) Chemical Hazards Information Response System
    c) Material Safety Data Sheet
    d) CHEMTREC

15. Which of the following is an inaccurate statement regarding radiation?
    a) X-rays are a significant source of radiation.
    b) More than 80 percent of our exposure to radiation comes from natural sources.
    c) Radiation comes from outer space, the ground, and even from our own bodies.
    d) There was no radiation present prior to 1944.

16. If you have a diagnostic X-ray, then you have been:
    a) Externally irradiated
    b) Contaminated
    c) Made radioactive
    d) Exposed to potentially lethal doses of radiation

17. Alpha and beta particles and gamma rays are examples of:
    a) Atoms
    b) Ionizing radiation
    c) Neutrons
    d) Isotopes

18. The SI unit for quantity of radioactive materials is:
    a) Becquerel
    b) Millicurie
    c) Microcurie
    d) Curie

19. How is the exposure rate generally expressed?
    a) In Roentgens Per Hour
    b) In Gray
    c) In Radiation Absorbed Dose
    d) In Microcurie

20. How can you reduce the exposure to ionizing radiation?
    a) Stand at least two inches away from the radiation source.
    b) Spend as little time as possible in a radiation field.
    c) Avoid standing next to a metal doorway.
    d) Don't live near a nuclear facility.

APPENDIX C: "None/Some/Good Table"

Response of Radiation Monitoring Instruments to Normalized Risk Quantities of Radionuclides

K.F. Eckerman
Oakridge National Laboratory
Health and Safety Research Division
Oak Ridge, TN 37831

A.W. Carriker
US Department of Transportation
Research and Special Programs Administration
400 Seventh Street SW
Washington, DC 20590

March 1992

Prepared by Sandia National Laboratories, Albuquerque, NM 87185
and Livermore, CA 94550 for the US Department of Energy under
Contract DE-AC04-76DP00789

Part III
Department of Transportation
Research and Special Programs Administration
49 CFR Part 171, et al.
Hazardous Materials, Transportation Regulations;
Compatibility with Regulation of the International Atomic Energy Agency;
Final Rule
September 28, 1995

M = minute   D = day   G = good

H = hour   Y = year   S = some   N = none

			700 Shield		715
Nuclide	**Half-life**	**Radiation**	**Open**	**Closed**	
Actinium					
Ac-225	*10.0 D*	αβγ	*G*	*S*	*N*
Ac-227	*21.773 Y*	αβγ	*N*	*N*	*N*
Ac-228	*6.13 H*	βγ	*G*	*G*	*S*
Aluminum					
Al-26	*7.16E5 Y*	βγ	*G*	*G*	*G*
Americium					
Am-241	*432.2 Y*	αβγ	*N*	*N*	*N*
Am-242m	*152 Y*	αβγ	*G*	*N*	*N*
Am-243	*7380 Y*	αβγ	*G*	*N*	*N*
Antimony					
Sb-122	*2.70 D*	βγ	*G*	*G*	*S*
Sb-124	*60.20 D*	βγ	*G*	*G*	*G*
Sb-125	*2.77 Y*	βγ	*G*	*G*	*S*
Sb-126	*12.4 D*	βγ	*G*	*G*	*S*
Argon					
Ar-37	*35.02 D*	βγ	*N*	*N*	*N*
Ar-39	*269 Y*	β	*G*	*N*	*N*
Ar-41	*1.827 H*	βγ	*G*	*G*	*S*
Arsenic					
As-72	*26.0 H*	βγ	*G*	*G*	*S*
As-73	*80.30 D*	βγ	*G*	*G*	*G*
As-74	*17.76 D*	βγ	*G*	*G*	*S*
As-76	*26.32 H*	βγ	*G*	*G*	*N*
As-77	*38.8 H*	βγ	*G*	*S*	*N*
Astatine					
At-211	*7.214 H*	αβγ	*G*	*G*	*S*
Barium					
Ba-131	*11.8 D*	βγ	*G*	*G*	*G*
Ba-133	*10.74 Y*	βγ	*G*	*G*	*G*
Ba-133m	*38.9 H*	βγ	*G*	*G*	*N*
Ba-140	*12.74 D*	βγ	*G*	*G*	*S*

Response of Radiation Monitoring Instruments to Normalized Risk Quantities of Radionuclides

| Nuclide | Half-life | Radiation | 700 Shield | | 715 |
			Open	Closed	
Berkelium					
Bk-247	*1380 Y*	αβγ	*N*	*N*	*N*
Bk-249	*320 D*	αβγ	*N*	*N*	*N*
Beryllium					
Be-7	*53.3 D*	βγ	*G*	*G*	*G*
Be-10	*1.6E6 Y*	β	*G*	*N*	*N*
Bismuth					
Bi-205	*15.31 D*	βγ	*G*	*G*	*S*
Bi-206	*6.243 D*	βγ	*G*	*G*	*G*
Bi-207	*38 Y*	βγ	*G*	*G*	*G*
Bi-210	*5.012 D*	βγ	*G*	*N*	*N*
Bi-210m	*3.0E6 Y*	αβγ	*G*	*G*	*N*
BI-212	*60.55 M*	αβγ	*G*	*G*	*N*
Bromine					
Br-76	*16.2 H*	βγ	*G*	*G*	*S*
Br-77	*56 H*	βγ	*G*	*G*	*G*
Br-82	*35.30 H*	βγ	*G*	*G*	*S*
Cadmium					
Cd-109	*464 D*	βγ	*G*	*G*	*S*
Cd-113M	*13.6 Y*	β	*G*	*N*	*N*
Cd-115	*53.46 H*	βγ	*G*	*G*	*S*
Cd-115m	*44.6 D*	βγ	*G*	*S*	*N*
Calcium					
Ca-41	*1.4E5 Y*	βγ	*N*	*N*	*N*
Ca-45	*163 D*	βγ	*G*	*N*	*N*
Ca-47	*4.53 D*	βγ	*G*	*G*	*S*
Californium					
Cf-248	*333.5 D*	αβγ	*N*	*N*	*N*
Cf-249	*350.6 Y*	αβγ	*N*	*N*	*N*
Cf-251	*13.08 Y*	αβγ	*N*	*N*	*N*
Cf-252	*898 Y*	αβγ	*N*	*N*	*N*
Cf-253	*17.81 Y*	αβγ	*G*	*N*	*N*
Cf-254	*60.5 D*	αβγ	*S*	*S*	*N*
Carbon					
C-11	*20.38 M*	βγ	*G*	*S*	*N*
C-14	*5730 Y*	βγ	*N*	*N*	*N*

Nuclide	Half-life	Radiation	700 Shield		715
			Open	Closed	
Cerium					
Ce-139	137.66 D	βγ	G	G	G
Ce-141	32.501 D	βγ	G	G	N
Ce-143	33.0 H	βγ	G	G	S
Ce-144	284.3 D	βγ	G	G	N
Cesium					
Cs-129	32.06 H	βγ	G	G	G
Cs-131	9.69 D	βγ	G	G	G
Cs-132	6.475 D	βγ	G	G	G
Cs-134	2.062 Y	βγ	G	G	G
Cs-134m	2.90 H	βγ	G	G	S
Cs-135	2.3E6 Y	β	G	N	N
Cs-136	13.1 D	βγ	G	G	S
Cs-137	30.0 Y	βγ	G	G	S
Chlorine					
Cl-36	3.01E5 Y	βγ	G	N	N
Cl-38	37.21 M	βγ	G	G	N
Chromium					
Cr-51	27.704 D	βγ	G	G	G
Cobalt					
Co-56	78.76 D	βγ	G	G	G
Co-57	270.9 D	βγ	G	G	G
Co-58	70.80 D	βγ	G	G	G
Co-58m	9.15 H	βγ	S	N	N
Co-60	5.271 Y	βγ	G	G	G
Copper					
Cu-64	12.701 H	βγ	G	G	G
Cu-67	61.86 H	βγ	G	G	S
Curium					
Cm-240	27 D	αβγ	N	N	N
Cm-241	32.8 D	αβγ	G	G	G
Cm-242	162.8 D	αβγ	N	N	N
Cm-243	28.5 Y	αβγ	N	N	N
Cm-244	18.11 Y	αβγ	N	N	N
Cm-245	8500 Y	αβγ	N	N	N
Cm-246	4730 Y	αβγ	N	N	N
Cm-247	1.56E7 Y	αβγ	G	N	N
Cm-248	3.39E5 Y	αβγ	N	N	N

Nuclide	Half-life	Radiation	700 Shield		715
			Open	Closed	
Dysprosium					
Dy-159	*144.4 D*	βγ	*G*	*G*	*G*
Dy-165	*2.334 H*	βγ	*G*	*S*	*N*
Dy-166	*81.6 H*	βγ	*G*	*G*	*N*
Erbium					
Er-169	*9.3 D*	βγ	*G*	*N*	*N*
Er-171	*7.52 H*	βγ	*G*	*G*	*S*
Europium					
Eu-147	*24 D*	αβγ	*G*	*G*	*G*
Eu-148	*5.5 D*	αβγ	*G*	*G*	*G*
Eu-149	*93.1 D*	βγ	*G*	*G*	*G*
Eu-152	*13.33 Y*	βγ	*G*	*G*	*G*
Eu-152m	*9.32 H*	βγ	*G*	*G*	*G*
Eu-154	*8.8 Y*	βγ	*G*	*G*	*S*
Eu-155	*4.96 Y*	βγ	*G*	*G*	*S*
Eu-156	*15.19 D*	βγ	*G*	*G*	*S*
Fluorine					
F-18	*107.77 M*	βγ	*G*	*G*	*S*
Gadolinium					
Gd-146	*48.3 D*	βγ	*G*	*G*	*G*
Gd-153	*242 D*	βγ	*G*	*G*	*G*
Gd-159	*18.56 H*	βγ	*G*	*G*	*N*
Gallium					
Ga-67	*78.26 H*	βγ	*G*	*G*	*G*
Ga-68	*68.0 M*	βγ	*G*	*G*	*N*
Ga-72	*14.1 H*	βγ	*G*	*G*	*G*
Germanium					
Ge-68	*288 D*	βγ	*G*	*G*	*S*
Ge-71	*11.8 D*	βγ	*G*	*N*	*S*
Ge-77	*11.30 H*	βγ	*G*	*G*	*S*
Gold					
Au-193	*17.65 H*	βγ	*G*	*G*	*G*
Au-194	*39.5 H*	βγ	*G*	*G*	*G*
Au-195	*183 D*	βγ	*G*	*G*	*G*
Au-198	*2.696 D*	βγ	*G*	*G*	*S*
Au-199	*3.139 D*	βγ	*G*	*G*	*S*

Nuclide	Half-life	Radiation	700 Shield		715
			Open	**Closed**	
Hafnium					
Hf-172	*1.87 Y*	βγ	*G*	*G*	*S*
Hf-175	*70 D*	βγ	*G*	*G*	*G*
Hf-181	*42.4 D*	βγ	*G*	*G*	*S*
Hf-182	*9E6 Y*	βγ	*G*	*G*	*N*
Holmium					
Ho-166	*26.80 H*	βγ	*G*	*S*	*N*
Ho-166m	*1.20E3 Y*	βγ	*G*	*G*	*S*
Hydrogen					
H-3	*12.35 Y*	β	*N*	*N*	*N*
Indium					
In-111	*2.83 D*	βγ	*G*	*G*	*G*
In-113m	*1.658 H*	βγ	*G*	*G*	*S*
In-114m	*49.51 D*	βγ	*G*	*G*	*N*
In-115m	*4.486 H*	βγ	*G*	*G*	*S*
Iodine					
I-123	*13.2 H*	βγ	*G*	*G*	*G*
I-124	*4.18 D*	βγ	*G*	*G*	*G*
I-125	*60.14 D*	βγ	*G*	*S*	*S*
I-126	*13.0 D*	βγ	*G*	*G*	*S*
I-129	*1.57E7 Y*	βγ	*G*	*G*	*G*
I-131	*8.04 D*	βγ	*G*	*G*	*S*
I-132	*2.30 H*	βγ	*G*	*G*	*S*
I-133	*20.8 H*	βγ	*G*	*G*	*S*
I-134	*52.6 M*	βγ	*G*	*G*	*S*
I-135	*6.61 H*	βγ	*G*	*G*	*S*
Iridium					
Ir-189	*13.3 D*	βγ	*G*	*G*	*G*
Ir-190	*12.1 D*	βγ	*G*	*G*	*S*
Ir-192	*74.02 D*	βγ	*G*	*G*	*S*
Ir-194	*19.15 H*	βγ	*G*	*G*	*N*
Iron					
Fe-52	*8.275 H*	βγ	*G*	*G*	*S*
Fe-55	*2.7 Y*	βγ	*N*	*N*	*N*
Fe-59	*44.529 D*	βγ	*G*	*G*	*G*
Fe-60	*1E5 Y*	βγ	*G*	*S*	*N*

Nuclide	Half-life	Radiation	700 Shield		715
			Open	Closed	
Krypton					
Kr-81	*2.1E5 Y*	βγ	*G*	*G*	*G*
Kr-85	*10.72 Y*	βγ	*G*	*G*	*N*
Kr-85m	*4.48 H*	βγ	*G*	*G*	*G*
Kr-87	*76.3 M*	βγ	*G*	*G*	*N*
Lanthanum					
La-137	*6E4 Y*	βγ	*G*	*S*	*S*
La-140	*40.272 H*	βγ	*G*	*G*	*S*
Lead					
Pb-201	*9.4 H*	βγ	*G*	*G*	*G*
Pb-202	*3E5 Y*	βγ	*G*	*G*	*G*
Pb-203	*52.05 H*	βγ	*G*	*G*	*G*
PB-205	*1.43E7 Y*	βγ	*G*	*N*	*S*
Pb-210	*22.3 Y*	αβγ	*G*	*N*	*N*
Pb-212	*1064 H*	αβγ	*G*	*G*	*S*
Lutetium					
Lu-172	*6.70 D*	βγ	*G*	*G*	*G*
Lu-173	*1.37 Y*	βγ	*G*	*G*	*G*
Lu-174	*3.31 Y*	βγ	*G*	*G*	*S*
Lu-174m	*142 D*	βγ	*G*	*G*	*G*
Lu-177	*6.71 D*	βγ	*G*	*G*	*N*
Magnesium					
Mg-28	*20.91*	βγ	*G*	*G*	*S*
Manganese					
Mn-52	*5.591 D*	βγ	*G*	*G*	*G*
Mn-53	*3.7E6 Y*	βγ	*N*	*N*	*N*
Mn-54	*312.5 D*	βγ	*G*	*G*	*G*
Mn-56	*2.5785 H*	βγ	*G*	*G*	*S*
Mercury					
Hg-194	*260 Y*	βγ	*G*	*G*	*G*
Hg-195m	*41.6 H*	βγ	*G*	*G*	*G*
Hg-197	*64.1 H*	βγ	*G*	*G*	*G*
Hg-197m	*23.8 H*	βγ	*G*	*G*	*S*
Hg-203	*46.60 D*	βγ	*G*	*G*	*S*
Mixed Fission Products					
MFP		βγ	*G*	*G*	*S*

Nuclide	Half-life	Radiation	700 Shield Open	700 Shield Closed	715
Molybdenum					
Mo-93	3.5E3 Y	βγ	G	N	G
Mo-99	66.0 H	βγ	G	G	S
Neodymium					
Nd-147	10.98 D	βγ	G	G	N
Nd-149	1.73 H	βγ	G	G	N
Neptunium					
Np-235	396.1 D	αβγ	G	G	G
Np-237	2.14E6 Y	αβγ	N	N	N
Np-239	2.355 D	βγ	G	G	S
Nickel					
Ni-59	7.5E4 Y	βγ	N	N	N
Ni-63	96 Y	β	N	N	N
Ni-65	2.520 H	βγ	G	G	N
Niobium					
Nb-93m	13.6 Y	βγ	G	N	S
Nb-94	2.03E4 Y	βγ	G	G	G
Nb-95	35.15 D	βγ	G	G	S
Nb-97	72.1 M	βγ	G	G	N
Nitrogen					
N-13	9.965 M	βγ	N	N	N
Osmium					
Os-185	94 D	βγ	G	G	G
Os-191	15.4 D	βγ	G	G	S
Os-191m	13.03 H	βγ	G	G	G
Os-193	30.0 H	βγ	G	G	N
Os-194	6.0 Y	βγ	G	G	N
Palladium					
Pd-103	16.96 D	βγ	G	G	G
Pd-107	65E6 Y	β	N	N	N
Pd-109	13.427 H	βγ	G	S	N
Phosphorus					
P-32	14.29 D	β	G	N	N
P-33	25.4 D	β	G	N	N

| Nuclide | Half-life | Radiation | 700 Shield | | 715 |
			Open	Closed	
Platinum					
Pt-188	*10.2 D*	βγ	*G*	*G*	*S*
Pt-191	*2.8 D*	βγ	*G*	*G*	*G*
Pt-193	*50 Y*	βγ	*G*	*N*	*G*
Pt-195m	*4.02 D*	βγ	*G*	*G*	*S*
Pt-197	*18.3 H*	βγ	*G*	*G*	*N*
Pt-197m	*94.4 M*	βγ	*G*	*G*	*N*
Plutonium					
Pu-236	*2.81 Y*	αβγ	*N*	*N*	*N*
Pu-237	*45.3 D*	αβγ	*G*	*G*	*G*
Pu-238	*87.74 Y*	αβγ	*N*	*N*	*N*
Pu-239	*24065 Y*	αβγ	*N*	*N*	*N*
Pu-240	*6537 Y*	αβγ	*N*	*N*	*N*
Pu-241	*14.4 Y*	αβγ	*N*	*N*	*N*
Pu-242	*3.76E5 Y*	αβγ	*N*	*N*	*N*
Pu-244	*8.26E7 Y*	αβγ	*G*	*N*	*N*
Polonium					
Po-210	*1.38.38 D*	αβγ	*N*	*N*	*N*
Potassium					
K-42	*12.36 H*	βγ	*G*	*G*	*N*
K-43	*22.6 H*	βγ	*G*	*G*	*S*
Praseodymium					
Pr-142	*19.13 H*	βγ	*G*	*G*	*N*
Pr-143	*13.56 D*	βγ	*G*	*N*	*N*
Promethium					
Pm-143	*265 D*	βγ	*G*	*G*	*G*
Pm-144	*363 D*	βγ	*G*	*G*	*G*
Pm-145	*17.7 Y*	βγ	*G*	*G*	*S*
Pm-147	*2.6234 Y*	βγ	*G*	*N*	*N*
Pm-148m	*41.3 D*	βγ	*G*	*G*	*G*
Pm-149	*53.08 H*	βγ	*G*	*S*	*N*
Pm-151	*28.40 H*	βγ	*G*	*G*	*S*
Protactinium					
Pa-230	*17.4 D*	αβγ	*G*	*G*	*S*
Pa-231	*3.276E4 Y*	αβγ	*N*	*N*	*N*
Pa-233	*27.0 Y*	βγ	*G*	*G*	*S*

| Nuclide | Half-life | Radiation | 700 Shield | | 715 |
			Open	Closed	
Radium					
Ra-223	11.434 D	αβγ	G	S	N
Ra-224	3.66 D	αβγ	G	G	N
Ra-225	14.8 D	αβγ	G	S	N
Ra-226	1600 Y	αβγ	G	G	N
Ra-228	5.75 Y	βγ	G	G	N
Radon					
Rn-222	3.8235 D	αβγ	G	S	N
Rhenium					
Re-184	38.0 D	βγ	G	G	G
Re-184m	165 D	βγ	G	G	G
Re-186	90.64 H	βγ	G	G	N
Re-187	5E10 Y	β	N	N	N
Re-188	16.98 Y	βγ	G	G	N
Re-189	24.3 H	βγ	G	G	N
Rhodium					
Rh-99	16 D	βγ	G	G	G
Rh-101	3.2 Y	βγ	G	G	G
Rh-102	2.9 Y	βγ	G	G	G
Rh-102m	207 D	βγ	G	G	G
Rh-103m	56.12 M	βγ	G	N	N
Rh-105	35.36 H	βγ	G	G	N
Rubidium					
Rb-81	4.58 H	βγ	G	G	S
Rb-83	86.2 D	βγ	G	G	G
Rb-84	32.77 D	βγ	G	G	G
Rb-86	18.66 D	βγ	G	G	N
Rb-87	4.7E10 Y	β	G	N	N
Ruthenium					
Ru-97	2.9 D	βγ	G	G	G
Ru-103	39.28D	βγ	G	G	S
Ru-105	4.44 H	βγ	G	G	S
Ru-106	368.2 D	βγ	G	G	N
Samarium					
Sm-145	340 D	α	G	G	G
Sm-147	1.06E11 Y	βγ	N	N	N
Sm-151	90 Y	βγ	N	N	N
Sm-153	46.7 H	βγ	G	G	N

Nuclide	Half-life	Radiation	700 Shield		715
			Open	Closed	
Scandium					
Sc-44	*3.927 H*	βγ	*G*	*G*	*S*
Sc-46	*83.83 D*	βγ	*G*	*G*	*G*
Sc-47	*3.351 D*	βγ	*G*	*G*	*S*
Sc-48	*43.7 H*	βγ	*G*	*G*	*S*
Selenium					
Se-75	*119.8 D*	βγ	*G*	*G*	*G*
Se-79	*65000 Y*	β	*N*	*N*	*N*
Silicon					
Si-31	*157.3 M*	βγ	*G*	*N*	*N*
Si-32	*450 Y*	β	*G*	*N*	*N*
Silver					
Ag-105	*41.0 D*	βγ	*G*	*G*	*G*
Ag-108m	*127 Y*	βγ	*G*	*G*	*G*
Ag-110m	*249.9 D*	βγ	*G*	*G*	*G*
Ag-111	*7.45 D*	βγ	*G*	*G*	*N*
Sodium					
Na-22	*2.602 Y*	βγ	*G*	*G*	*G*
Na-24	*15.00 H*	βγ	*G*	*G*	*S*
Strontium					
Sr-82	*25 D*	βγ	*G*	*G*	*S*
Sr-85	*64.84 D*	βγ	*G*	*G*	*G*
Sr-85m	*69.5 M*	βγ	*G*	*G*	*S*
Sr-87m	*2.805 H*	βγ	*G*	*G*	*S*
Sr-89	*50.5 D*	βγ	*G*	*N*	*N*
Sr-90	*29.12 Y*	βγ	*G*	*N*	*N*
Sr-91	*9.5 H*	βγ	*G*	*G*	*S*
Sr-92	*2.71 H*	βγ	*G*	*G*	*S*
Sulfur					
S-35	*87.44 D*	β	*N*	*N*	*N*
Tantalum					
Ta-179	*664.9 D*	βγ	*G*	*G*	*G*
Ta-182	*115.0 D*	βγ	*G*	*G*	*S*

Nuclide	Half-life	Radiation	700 Shield		715
			Open	Closed	
Technetium					
Tc-95m	*61 D*	βγ	*G*	*G*	*G*
Tc-96	*4.28D*	βγ	*G*	*G*	*G*
Tc-96m	*51.5 m*	βγ	*S*	*S*	*N*
Tc-97	*2.6E6 Y*	βγ	*G*	*N*	*G*
Tc-97m	*87 D*	βγ	*G*	*G*	*G*
Tc-98	*4.2E6 Y*	βγ	*G*	*G*	*G*
Tc-99	*2.13E5 Y*	β	*G*	*N*	*N*
Tc-99m	*6.02 H*	βγ	*G*	*G*	*G*
Tellurium					
Te-121	*17 D*	βγ	*G*	*G*	*G*
Te-121m	*154 D*	βγ	*G*	*G*	*G*
Te-123m	*119.7 D*	βγ	*G*	*G*	*G*
Te-125m	*58 D*	βγ	*G*	*G*	*G*
Te-127	*9.35 H*	βγ	*G*	*S*	*N*
Te-127m	*109 D*	βγ	*G*	*S*	*N*
Te-129	*69.6 M*	βγ	*G*	*S*	*N*
Te-129m	*33.6 D*	βγ	*G*	*G*	*N*
Te-131m	*30 H*	βγ	*G*	*G*	*S*
Te-132	*78.2 H*	βγ	*G*	*G*	*G*
Terbium					
Tb-157	*150 Y*	βγ	*G*	*S*	*N*
Tb-158	*150 Y*	βγ	*G*	*G*	*S*
Tb-160	*72.3 D*	βγ	*G*	*G*	*S*
Thallium					
Tl-200	*26.1 H*	βγ	*G*	*G*	*S*
Tl-201	*3.044 D*	βγ	*G*	*G*	*G*
Tl-202	*12.23 D*	βγ	*G*	*G*	*S*
Tl-204	*3.779 Y*	βγ	*G*	*S*	*N*
Thorium					
Th-227	*18.718 D*	αβγ	*G*	*S*	*N*
Th-228	*1.9131 Y*	αβγ	*G*	*N*	*N*
Th-229	*7340 Y*	αβγ	*S*	*N*	*N*
Th-230	*7.7E4 Y*	αβγ	*N*	*N*	*N*
Th-231	*25.52 H*	αβγ	*G*	*G*	*S*
Th-232	*1.405E10 Y*	αβγ	*N*	*N*	*N*
Th-234	*24.10 D*	αβγ	*G*	*S*	*N*

Nuclide	Half-life	Radiation	700 Shield Open	700 Shield Closed	715
Thulium					
Tm-167	*9.24 D*	βγ	*G*	*G*	*G*
Tm-170	*128.6 D*	βγ	*G*	*S*	*N*
Tm-171	*1.92 Y*	βγ	*G*	*S*	*N*
Tin					
Sn-113	*115.1 D*	βγ	*G*	*G*	*G*
Sn-117m	*13.61 D*	βγ	*G*	*G*	*S*
Sn-119m	*293.0 D*	βγ	*G*	*G*	*G*
Sn-121	*55 Y*	βγ	*G*	*N*	*N*
Sn-123	*129.2 D*	βγ	*G*	*S*	*N*
Sn-125	*9.64 D*	βγ	*G*	*G*	*N*
Sn-126	*1.0E5 Y*	βγ	*G*	*G*	*S*
Titanium					
Ti-44	*47.3 Y*	βγ	*G*	*G*	*S*
Tungsten (Wolfram)					
W-178	*21.7 D*	βγ	*G*	*G*	*S*
W-181	*121.2 D*	βγ	*G*	*G*	*G*
W-185	*75.1 D*	βγ	*G*	*N*	*N*
W-187	*23.9 H*	βγ	*G*	*G*	*S*
W-188	*69.4 D*	βγ	*G*	*G*	*N*
Uranium					
U-230	*20.8 D*	αβγ	*N*	*N*	*N*
U-232	*72 Y*	αβγ	*N*	*N*	*N*
U-233	*1.585E5 Y*	αβγ	*N*	*N*	*N*
U-234	*2.445E5 Y*	αβγ	*N*	*N*	*N*
U-235	*703.8E6 Y*	αβγ	*G*	*G*	*S*
U-236	*2.3415E7 Y*	αβγ	*N*	*N*	*N*
U-238	*4.468E9 Y*	αβγ	*G*	*N*	*N*
U-nat[1]		αβγ	*G*	*N*	*S*
U-nat[2]		αβγ	*G*	*S*	*N*
U-nat[3]		αβγ	*S*	*N*	*N*
Vanadium					
V-48	*16.238 D*	βγ	*G*	*G*	*S*
V-49	*330 D*	βγ	*N*	*N*	

Nuclide	Half-life	Radiation	700 Shield		715
			Open	Closed	
Xenon					
Xe-122	*20.1 H*	βγ	*G*	*G*	*S*
Xe-123	*2.08 H*	βγ	*G*	*G*	*N*
Xe-127	*36.41 D*	βγ	*G*	*G*	*G*
Xe-131m	*11.9 D*	βγ	*G*	*G*	*G*
Xe-133	*.245 D*	βγ	*G*	*G*	*G*
Xe-135	*9.09 H*	βγ	*G*	*G*	*G*
Ytterbium					
Yb-169	*32.01 D*	βγ	*G*	*G*	*G*
Yb-175	*4.19 D*	βγ	*G*	*G*	*N*
Yttrium					
Y-87	*80.3 H*	βγ	*G*	*G*	*G*
Y-88	*106.64 D*	βγ	*G*	*G*	*G*
Y-90	*64.0 H*	βγ	*G*	*N*	*N*
Y-91	*58.51 D*	βγ	*G*	*S*	*N*
Y-91m	*49.71 M*	βγ	*G*	*G*	*S*
Y-92	*3.54 H*	βγ	*G*	*G*	*S*
Y-93	*10.1 H*	βγ	*G*	*G*	*N*
Zinc					
Zn-65	*243.9 D*	βγ	*G*	*G*	*G*
Zn-69	*57 M*	βγ	*G*	*N*	*N*
Zn-69m	*13.76 H*	βγ	*G*	*G*	*S*
Zirconium					
Zr-88	*83.4 D*	βγ	*G*	*G*	*G*
Zr-93	*1.53E6 Y*	β	*N*	*N*	*N*
Zr-95	*63.98 D*	βγ	*G*	*G*	*G*
Zr-97	*16.90 H*	βγ	*G*	*G*	*S*

[1] Computed response for natural Uranium

[2] Observed response for a 1 kg compact pile of yellowcake

[3] Observed response from a 1 kg cube of depleted uranium metal

Appendix D: GLOSSARY

Absorbed Dose

The energy imparted to matter by ionizing radiation per unit mass of irradiated material at the place of interest. The unit of absorbed dose is the radiation absorbed dose (rad).

Absorption

The passing of a substance into the circulatory system of the body. Also used specifically to refer to entry of toxicants through the skin. In radiological sciences, absorption is the imparting of some or all of the energy contained in ionizing radiation as it passes through matter.

Activity

The rate of decay of radioactive material, expressed as the average number of nuclear disintegration per second in a given quantity of radioactive material.

Acute Exposure

An exposure to a toxic substance which occurs in a short or single time period.

Acute Radiation Syndrome

A disease state that occurs in hours to months as damage caused by ionizing radiation to organs and tissues is expressed clinically. The disease is divided into 4 stages based on time. The first is the prodrome, followed by the latent, manifest illness and recovery/death stages (see below).

Acute Toxicity

Any poisonous effect produced by a single short-term exposure. The LD_{50} of a substance (the lethal dose at which 50 percent of test animals succumb to the toxicity of the chemicals) is typically used as a measure of its acute toxicity.

Additive Effect

A biological response to exposure to multiple chemicals which is equal to the sum of the effects of the individual agents.

Adsorption

The bonding of chemicals to soil particles or other surfaces.

Aerosol

A solid particle or liquid droplet suspended in air. An aerosol is larger than a molecule and can be filtered from the air.

Antagonism

The situation in which two chemicals interfere with each other's actions, or one chemical interferes with the action of the other.

Alpha Particle	A specific particle ejected spontaneously from the nucleus of some radioactive elements. It is identical to a helium nucleus (He; 2 protons and 2 neutrons), which has an atomic mass of 4 and an electrostatic charge of +2. It has low penetrating power and a short range. The most energetic alpha particle will generally fail to penetrate the skin. The danger occurs when matter containing alpha-emitting radionuclides are introduced into the body.
Aquifer	An underground bed, or layer, of earth, gravel, or porous storage that contains water.
Asphyxiants	Chemicals that deprive cells of an individual of oxygen needed to sustain metabolism.
Atom	The smallest particle of an element which cannot be divided or broken up by chemical means. It consists of a central core called the nucleus, which contains protons and neutrons. Electrons revolve in orbits around the nucleus.
Atomic Number	The number of protons in the nucleus of an atom. Each chemical element has its characteristic atomic number, and the atomic numbers of the known elements form a complete series from 1 (hydrogen) to 103 (lawrencium). Elements with atomic numbers 104 and 105 are presently unnamed.
Background Radiation	The radiation in the environment, including cosmic rays and radiation from the naturally radioactive elements, both outside and inside the bodies of animals and humans. It is also called natural radiation. Man-made sources of radioactivity contribute to total background radiation levels. Approximately 90 percent of the background radiation from man-made sources is related to the use of ionizing radiation in medicine and dentistry.
Beta Particle	A small particle ejected spontaneously from a nucleus of a radioactive element. It has the mass of an electron and has a charge of minus one. It has a medium or intermediate penetrating power and a range of up to a few meters in air. Beta particles will penetrate only a fraction of an inch of skin tissue, and is capable of damaging the skin.
Biodegradable	Capable of decomposing through the action of microorganisms.

Boiling Point	The temperature at which a liquid will start to become a gas, and boil. A chemical with a low boiling point can boil and evaporate quickly. If a material that is flammable also has a low boiling point, a special fire hazard exists.
Carcinogen	A chemical or physical agent that is capable of causing a cell to undergo malignant transformation to a cancer cell.
Central Nervous System Depressants	Toxicants that depress the activity of the central nervous system (CNS), diminishing responsiveness and alertness.
CERCLA	The Comprehensive Environmental Response, Compensation, and Liability Act of 1980—the Federal statute that authorized "Superfund." Administered by EPA, the law provides funding for cleanups and emergency response actions for hazardous substances at the worst hazardous waste sites in the United States. CERCLA is also significant because it set the first criteria for notification of emergencies involving hazardous substances.
Charged Particle	An elementary particle that carries a positive or negative electrical charge.
CHEMTREC	Chemical Transportation Emergency Center, a service operated by the Chemical Manufacturers Association to provide information and other assistance to emergency responders.
Chronic Exposure	Process by which small amounts of toxic substances are taken into the body over an extended period.
Controlled Area	An area where entry, activities, and exit are controlled to assure protection and prevent the spread of contamination.
Corrosive	A chemical that destroys or irreversibly alters living tissue by direct chemical action at the site of contact. Another name for acids.
Cosmic Rays	High-energy particulate and electromagnetic radiation which originate outside the earth's atmosphere.
Curie	The basic measuring unit used to describe the amount of radioactivity in a sample of material. One curie is equal to 37 billion disintegrations per second. Symbol Ci.
Decontamination	The process of removing or neutralizing contaminants that have accumulated on personnel, structures, area, and equipment.

Dermal Exposure

Exposure to toxic substances by entry though the skin.

Detector

A material or device that is sensitive to radiation and can produce a response signal suitable for measurement and analysis. A radiation detection instrument.

Dose

A general term for denoting the quantity of radiation or energy absorbed. If unqualified, it refers to absorbed dose. For special purposes, it must be appropriately qualified. If used to represent exposure expressed in roentgens, it is a measure of the total amount of ionization that the quantity of radiation could produce in air.

Dose Equivalent

A quantity of measurement used in radiation protection. This term expresses all forms of radiation on a common scale for evaluating and comparing the effects of radiation in man. It is defined as the product of absorbed dose in rads and certain modifying factors. The unit of dose equivalent is the rem.

Dosimeter

A small, pocket-sized device used for personnel monitoring of radiation exposure. Measures total radiation dose to which it was exposed, much as an odometer measures total miles traveled.

Electromagnetic Radiation

A traveling energy wave that results from changing electric and magnetic fields. Familiar electromagnetic radiations range from those of short wave lengths, like X-rays and gamma rays, through the ultraviolet, visible light, and infrared regions, to radar and radio waves of relatively long wavelengths.

Electron

An elementary particle with a negative electrical charge. Electrons surround the positively charged nucleus and determine the chemical properties of the atom.

Evaporation Rate

The rate at which a chemical changes into a vapor. A chemical that evaporates quickly can be a more dangerous fire or health hazard.

Exercise

A simulated emergency condition carried out for the purpose of testing and evaluating the readiness of a community or organization to handle a particular type of emergency.

Explosive

A chemical that causes a sudden, almost instantaneous release of pressure, gas, and heat when subjected to sudden shock, pressure, or high temperatures.

Exposure

A quantity used to indicate the amount of ionization in air produced by beta or gamma radiation. The unit is the roentgen. For practical purposes, one roentgen is comparable to 1 rad or 1 rem for gamma radiation.

Extremely Hazardous Substance (EHS)
Any one of over 300 hazardous chemicals on a list compiled by EPA to provide a focus for State and local emergency planning activities.

Gamma Rays
Electromagnetic radiation of high energy, originating from atomic nuclei. Gamma rays are identical to x-rays of high energy, the only essential difference being that x-rays do not originate from atomic nuclei but are produced in other ways; for instance, by slowing down fast, high-energy electrons. Gamma rays are the most penetrating type of radiation and represent the major external hazard.

Geiger counter or G-M Meter
An instrument used to detect and measure radiation. The detecting element is a gas-filled chamber operated by a voltage whose electrical discharge will spread over the entire anode when triggered by a primary ionizing event.

Hazard Class
A group of materials, as designated by the Department of Transportation, that share a common major hazardous property such as radioactivity or flammability.

Hazardous Materials Response Team (HMRT)
A team of specially trained personnel who respond to a hazardous materials incident. The team performs various response actions including assessment, firefighting, rescue, and containment; they are **not** responsible for cleanup operations following the incident.

Incident Commander
The person in charge of on-scene coordination of a response to an incident, usually a senior officer in a fire department.

Inverse Square Law
The relationship which states that the change in gamma radiation intensity is inversely proportional to the square of the change in distance from a point source.

Inversion
An atmospheric condition caused by a layer of warm air preventing cool air trapped beneath it from rising, thus holding down pollutants that could otherwise be dispersed.

Ion
Atomic particle, atom, or chemical radical bearing an electrical charge, either positive or negative.

Ionization	The separation of a normally electrically neutral atom or molecule into electrically charged components. The term is also used to describe the degree or extent to which this separation occurs. Ionization is the removal of an electron (negative charge) from an atom or molecule, either directly or indirectly, leaving a positively charged ion. The separated electron and ion are referred to as an ion pair.
Ionizing Radiation	Electromagnetic radiation (x-ray and gamma ray photons) or particulate radiation capable of producing ions by direct or secondary processes.
Irradiation	Exposure to ionizing radiation.
Irritant	Chemicals which inflame living tissue by chemical action at the site of contact, causing pain or swelling.
Isotope	Forms of the same element having identical chemical properties, but differing in their atomic masses, due to different numbers of neutrons in their respective nuclei. For example, hydrogen has three isotopes, with one, two, and three atomic mass units. Each has one proton, and 0, 1, and 2 neutrons, respectively. H-1 is normal hydrogen, while H-2 and H-3 are commonly called deuterium and tritium, respectively. The first two of these are stable (nonradioactive), but the third, tritium, is a radioactive isotope.
LD$_{50}$	The calculated dosage of a material that would be fatal to 50% of an exposed population (Lethal Dose 50%).
Leachate	Material that pollutes water as it seeps through solid waste.
Leaching	The process by which water dissolves nutrient chemicals or contaminants and carries them away or moves them to a lower layer.
LEPC	Local Emergency Planning Committee.
LOAEL	The Lowest Observed Adverse Effect Level, i.e., the lowest dose which produces an observable adverse effect.
Mass Number	The sum of neutrons and protons in a nucleus, the mass number is the nearest whole number to an atom's atomic weight. For instance, the mass number for uranium-235 is 235.

Medium	The environmental vehicle by which a pollutant is carried to the receptor (e.g., air, surface water, soil, or groundwater).
Melting Point	The temperature at which a solid material changes to a liquid. Solid materials with low melting points should not be stored in hot areas.
Monitoring	Periodic or continuous determination of the amount of ionizing radiation or radioactive contamination present for purposes of health protection.
MSDS (Material Safety Data Sheet)	A worksheet required by the U.S. Occupational Safety and Health Administration (OSHA) containing information about hazardous chemicals in the workplace. MSDSs are used to fulfill part of the hazardous chemical inventory reporting requirements under the Emergency Planning and Community Right-to-Know Act.
Mutagen	A chemical or physical agent that induces a permanent change in the genetic material.
NOAEL	No Observable Adverse Effect Level.
Nucleus, Atomic	The small, positively charged core of an atom. It is only about 1/100,000 diameter of an atom but contains nearly all of the atom's mass. All nuclei contain both protons and neutrons, except for the nucleus of ordinary hydrogen which consists of a single proton.
Organic Compound	Chemicals that contain carbon. Volatile organic compounds vaporize at room temperature and pressure. They are found in many indoor sources, including many common household products and building materials.
OSHA	The Occupational Safety and Health Administration, part of the Department of Labor.
Pathway	A history of the flow of a pollutant from source to receptor, including qualitative descriptions of emission type, transport, medium, and exposure route.
PEL	Permissible Exposure Limits set by OSHA as a guide to acceptable levels of chemical exposure.
Poison	A chemical that, in relatively small amounts, is able to produce injury by chemical action when it comes in contact with a susceptible tissue.
Proton	An elementary particle with a single positive electrical charge. Protons are constituents of all nuclei. The atomic number of an atom is equal to the number of protons in its nucleus.

Rad	Radiation absorbed dose. A rad is the unit of absorbed dose. The rad is a measure of the energy imparted to matter by ionizing particles per unit mass of irradiated material at the place of interest. A rad is approximately equal to the absorbed dose in tissue when the exposure in air is one roentgen of medium-voltage gamma radiation.
Radiation	The propagation of energy through space or through a material medium as waves; for example, energy in the form of sound or electromagnetic waves. Radiation usually refers to electromagnetic radiation.
Radiation Accident	An accident in which there is an unintended exposure to ionizing radiation or radioactive contamination.
Radioactivity	The spontaneous emission of radiation, generally alpha or beta particles often accompanied by gamma rays, from the nucleus of an unstable atom. As a result of this emission, the radioactive atom is converted or decays into an atom of a different element that may or may not be radioactive.
Rem	Roentgen equivalent man - a special unit of radiation dose equivalent. The dose equivalent in rems is numerically equal to the absorbed dose multiplied by the quality factor, the distribution factor, and any necessary modifying factors.
Risk Assessment	Broadly defined as the scientific activity of evaluating the toxic properties of a chemical and the conditions of human exposure to it, with the objective of determining the probability that exposed humans will be adversely affected. Its four main components are: 1. **Hazard Identification**--Does the agent cause the effect? 2. **Dose-Response Assessment**--What is the relationship between the dose and its incidence in human beings? 3. **Exposure Assessment**--What exposures are experienced or anticipated, and under what conditions? 4. **Risk Characterization**--The total analysis producing an estimate of the incidence of the adverse effect in a given population.
Roentgen	The unit of exposure for x- or gamma radiation in air.
Runoff	Water from rain, snow melt, or irrigation that flows over the ground surface and returns to streams.
SARA	Superfund Amendments and Reauthorization Act of 1986.

Sealed Source	A radioactive source, sealed in an impervious container, which has sufficient mechanical strength to prevent contact with and dispersion of the radioactive material under the conditions of use and wear for which it was designed.
Solubility in Water	An indicator of the amount of a chemical that can be dissolved in water, shown as a percentage or as a description. A low percent of solubility (or a description of "slight" solubility or "low" solubility) means that only a small amount will dissolve in water. Knowing this may help firefighters or personnel cleaning a spill.
Specific Gravity	A comparison of the weight of the chemical to the weight of an equal volume of water. Chemicals with a specific gravity of less than 1 are lighter than water, while a specific gravity of more than 1 means the chemical is heavier than water. Most flammable liquids are lighter than water.
Survey Instrument	A portable instrument used for detecting and measuring radiation under varied physical conditions. The term covers a wide range of devices.
Synergistic Effect	A biological response to exposure to multiple chemicals which is greater than the sum of the effects of the individual agents.
Systemic Toxicants	Chemical compounds that affect entire organ systems, often operating far from the original site of entry.
Title III	The third part of SARA, also known as the Emergency Planning and Community Right-to-Know Act of 1986.
Toxicity	The degree of danger posed by a substance to animal or plant life.
Toxicology	The study of the adverse effects of chemicals on biological systems, and the assessment of the probability of their occurrence.
Transformation	The chemical alteration of a compound by processes such as reaction with other compounds or breakdown into component elements.
Transport	Hydrological, atmospheric, or other physical processes that convey pollutants through and across media from source to receptor.
Vapor Density	The measure of the heaviness of a chemical's vapor as compared to the weight of a similar amount of air. A vapor density of 1.0 is equal to air. Vapors that are heavier than air may build up in low-lying areas, such as along floors, in sewers, or in elevator shafts. Vapors that are lighter than air rise and may collect near the ceiling.

Vapor Pressure

The measure of how quickly a chemical liquid will evaporate. Chemicals with low boiling points have high vapor pressures. If a chemical with a high vapor pressure spills, there is an increased risk of explosion and a greater risk that workers will inhale toxic fumes.

Volatilization

Entry of contaminants into the atmosphere by evaporation from soil or water.

Whole-body (total) exposure

An exposure of the body to external radiation, where the entire body rather than an isolated part is irradiated. When a radioactive material is uniformly distributed throughout the body tissues rather than being concentrated in certain organs, the irradiation can be considered whole-body exposure.

Appendix E: Bibliography

Beatty, G.C. 1987. *Developing a Hospital Emergency Preparedness Program.* Chicago: American Hospital Association.

Cashman, J. 1995. *Hazardous Materials Emergencies: The Professional Response Team. Third Ed.* Technomic Publishing, Lancaster, PA.

FEMA, NFA. 1995. *Basic Life Support and Hazardous Materials Response.* Emmitsburg, MD.

FEMA, EMI. 1997. *Fundamentals Course for Radiological Monitors. Student Manual.* Emmitsburg, MD.

FEMA, EMI. 1997. *Fundamentals Course for Radiological Response Teams. Student Manual.* Emmitsburg, MD.

FEMA, EMI. 1990. *Hazardous Materials: A Citizen's Orientation Independent Study Course.* Emmitsburg, MD.

FEMA, EPA, DOT. 1993. *Hazardous Materials Workshop for Hospital Staff.* Emmitsburg, MD.

FEMA, EMI. 1984. *Hospital Emergency Management Department of Radiation Accidents.* Emmitsburg, MD (out of print).

FEMA Fax Information Line. 1993. *Hazardous Materials Backgrounder. Document #15092.*

International Atomic Energy Commission. 1988. *The Radiological Accident in Goiania.* Vienna.

Kuehl, A. (Ed.). 1994. *Prehospital Systems and Medical Oversight.* National Association of Emergency Physicians. Mosby-Year Book, Inc. St. Louis, MO.

NUREG-1458. 1992. *Emergency Response to a Highway Accident in Springfield, Massachusetts on December 16, 1991.* Washington, D.C.

Sherman, J. 1988. *Chemical Exposure and Disease.* Van Nostrand Reinhold. New York, NY.

U.S. Environmental Protection Agency. 1993. *Radiation: Risks and Realities.* Washington, D.C.

U.S. Nuclear Regulatory Commission. 1994. *Analysis and Evaluation of Operational Data.* Washington, D.C.

U.S. Nuclear Regulatory Commission. 1995. *Annual Report, 1994–FY1995, Nuclear Materials.* Office of Operational Data. Washington, D.C.

Varela, J. (Ed.). 1996. *Hazardous Materials Handbook for Emergency Responders.* Van Nostrand Reinhold. New York.